What is Ahead of Us?

G. D. H. Cole, Sir Arthur Salter, Wickham Steed, Sidney Webb, P. M. S. Blackett and Lancelot Hogben

Routledge
Taylor & Francis Group

First published in 1937
By George Allen & Unwin Ltd

This edition first published in 2023 by Routledge
4 Park Square, Milton Park, Abingdon, Oxon, OX14 4RN
and by Routledge
605 Third Avenue, New York, NY 10017

Routledge is an imprint of the Taylor & Francis Group, an informa business

Publisher's Note
The publisher has gone to great lengths to ensure the quality of this reprint but points out that some imperfections in the original copies may be apparent.

Disclaimer
The publisher has made every effort to trace copyright holders and welcomes correspondence from those they have been unable to contact.

A Library of Congress record exists under LCCN: 37009082

ISBN: 978-1-032-54869-2 (hbk)
ISBN: 978-1-003-42918-0 (ebk)
ISBN: 978-1-032-55139-5 (pbk)

Book DOI 10.4324/9781003429180

WHAT IS AHEAD OF US?

by

G. D. H. COLE

SIR ARTHUR SALTER

WICKHAM STEED

SIDNEY WEBB

P. M. S. BLACKETT

LANCELOT HOGBEN

LONDON

GEORGE ALLEN & UNWIN LTD

MUSEUM STREET

FIRST PUBLISHED IN 1937

CONTENTS

NOTE

In their long life the annual series of Fabian Lectures have only two or three times been published—and the first series of *Fabian Essays*, issued in 1889, is still in steady demand. The present book is based on a series which seemed too outstanding to be left unrecorded. Most of the lectures have, however, been substantially revised or even re-written for book publication. Mr. Webb's chapter is based on several lectures.

I

CAN CAPITALISM SURVIVE?

G. D. H. Cole

In this sorely tried and puzzled world of to-day, there is room for both short and long views; but there is hardly any room for views of what I may call the middle distance. Thus, in answering the question "Can Capitalism Survive?", it is possible to reply in terms of the immediate future, with some estimate of Capitalism's capacity for weathering the crisis which has been upon the world since 1929. Or it is possible to look much further ahead, and seek to measure Capitalism's capacity for long-run survival, in face of its manifest tendency to waste the resources of production by unemployment and to expose us and them to the devastating danger of war. What is not possible, or at any rate not profitable, is to take a middle view, and to estimate where Capitalism, either here or in the world as a whole, is likely to be in ten or in twenty years' time. For to-day the immediate outlook is so uncertain that we find ourselves compelled either to go back to first principles or to take very short views. We may maintain, as Socialists, that the contradictions of the capitalist system not merely remain unresolved, but become every year more glaring, and that more and more capitalist imperialism threatens year by year to tear itself and the world in pieces by universal war. But we have to recognize that, as far as the coming decade is concerned, these inherent tendencies of Capitalism are so intertwined with secondary tendencies, which manifest themselves daily in the current turmoil of world affairs, that however certain we may be of Capitalism's ultimate downfall, it is quite beyond our ability to say how or when the final crisis will arrive, or by what stages world history will move on to its next epoch, or even what the essential configurations of world affairs will be in ten or twenty years' time.

As Socialists, we are confident that Capitalism cannot survive indefinitely. No system does; for the basic social and economic forces are not of such a nature as to allow permanence. We are all Marxists enough to accept that, and to be well assured that Capitalism, like Feudalism before it, is destined some time to decay and dissolution. But when or how? That is the interesting part of the problem; and that is what I want principally to discuss.

The fundamental contradiction of Capitalism, according to the Marxists, lies in its inability to make use of the growing technical forces of productivity. It is constantly bringing these forces into being, constantly enlarging the world's technical capacity to produce wealth, constantly dangling before humanity the prospect of assured abundance. But despite the accelerated advance of the productive powers, mankind, over a large part of the capitalist world, has been growing of late not richer, but poorer; and there has appeared in one capitalist country a new kind of unemployment—no longer mere seasonal lack of work, no longer even more cyclical fluctuation in the demand for labour, but chronic unemployment, sheer redundancy of a part of the available labour force in relation to capitalist demand, sheer throwing of able-bodied workers on the scrapheap because, despite the continuance of poverty, Capitalism can find no use for the product of their hands.

Marx prophesied long ago that this would come to pass. Nearly a century ago, when Capitalism was still hurrying on to one conquest after another, he foresaw that in the end its very fecundity in invention would bring about its defeat, because it would become impossible within the limitations of the capitalist order to find consumers for the expanding wealth which the system would be technically competent to produce. He foresaw crises of growing magnitude, as the absolute expansion of the powers of production came more and more into conflict with the narrow limits of consumption. Capitalism, he held, could not allow consumption to keep pace with productivity because scarcity was for it the necessary condition of profit-making, and because it was of its very nature accumulative, so that it would tend always to invest in means of production more than could find an outlet through the consuming market. Means of production—that is, capital goods—are of no use at all unless they issue finally in a more ample flow of consumable goods and services. Saving and investment, unless they minister to future consumption, are sheer waste. It follows that, unless the will and the power to consume expand fast enough to take off the market all the goods and services which the resources of production allow to be produced, unemployment and crisis will inevitably arise. Factories and men will be thrown idle for want of a profitable market; and the system will be able to recover, and to address itself to a fresh advance, only when there has been a vast liquidation of unwanted productive power, that is, when many plants have been scrapped, many firms driven into bankruptcy, and very many workmen and technicians cast out of their jobs, to take their chance of re-employment when at last the crisis ends, and even then, very likely, to find their skill obsolete, and their best hope mere unskilled labour, if indeed there is any work still open to them at all.

Marx saw this nemesis coming upon Capitalism;

and for nearly a hundred years the defenders of Capitalism have had a fine time refuting him. They have exposed the fallacy of his argument by pointing to the huge strides forward which Capitalism has made since first he denounced its contradictions. They have shown how the workers in the capitalist countries, far from suffering increasing impoverishment, have grown materially very much better off; they have pointed to the undoubted huge enlargement of the market for consumable goods; and, while they have been unable to deny the continued liability of Capitalism to recurrent crises, they were arguing until only the other day that these crises, instead of becoming, as Marx anticipated, more severe, were in fact growing less formidable, and inflicting less distress either on the working classes or on the capitalists themselves.

Until only the other day—that is, until Capitalism plunged headlong into this latest and most devastating crisis of all. For no one can possibly deny that the world crisis which began with the Wall Street crash of 1929 has been severe beyond precedent, so that there was, for us Socialists and for panic-stricken business men as well, a strong temptation to mistake it for the final crisis of the capitalist system. We know now that it was not that; for one capitalist country after another, after staggering under the blows which were rained upon it between 1929 and 1932, has emerged into at least partial recovery, and in not one single country has Capitalism failed to survive. Despite the working example of Russian Socialism, there has been no Socialist revolution as a result of the crisis in any other country; for revolution and counter-revolution in Spain, while by no means unaffected by the world economic crisis, cannot be attributed to it in any direct sense.

The crisis has been unexampled in its severity; but Capitalism has not collapsed under its impact. British Capitalism, American Capitalism, French Capitalism, German Capitalism, and all the lesser Capitalisms of Holland, Italy, Belgium, and the rest, remain in effective possession of their respective countries and peoples. The great capitalist Empires have not dropped to pieces; on the contrary, some of them—Japan's and Italy's—have been enlarged by new conquests. Liquidation has taken place upon an unprecedented scale: debts have been repudiated right and left: many giants have been flung out of the capitalist heaven, and countless pigmies ground to powder. But in every country, except Russia, and perhaps (who knows?) Spain, the essential capitalist institutions remain intact. Capitalism has shown one thing very plainly indeed during the last few years—its toughness. It has shown itself "tough" in more senses than one—too tough to be easily eaten up, and "tough" enough to hit back ruthlessly at all who threaten its authority.

CAN CAPITALISM SURVIVE?

Oh, yes, the capitalist is a "tough guy," and we Socialists challenge him at our peril. When democracy threatens to bring him to book for his incompetent stewardship of economic affairs, he does not wait to be hit. He hits first—well below the belt. Italians, Germans, Austrians, and Spaniards have all good cause to know his methods; and in every Fascist country the eclipse of democracy has left Capitalism intact. The world crisis has failed to finish Capitalism by economic means; and when it has led to revolution, not Socialists but Fascists with capitalist money-bags at their service have made the revolutionary running.

There are, then, two aspects, distinct but closely connected, from which the question of Capitalism's power to survive has to be regarded. The first aspect is economic in a narrow sense. If not under this crisis, then under the next or the next after that, will Capitalism so break down economically as to be unable to carry on the work of keeping the people alive? Will the vast machine of capitalist production come to a dead stop because of the inherent economic contradictions of the profiteering system?

The second aspect is not purely economic, but economico-political. Will Capitalism, if it finds itself threatened either with economic collapse or with peaceful supersession by Socialist democracy, make in other countries, including our own, the same counter-revolution as it has made already in Italy and Germany? And, if it does, and the counter-revolution for the time succeeds, will it be possible for Capitalism, by sheer repression of the forces making for a new social system, to re-establish and stabilize its authority? Will this stabilization be possible in the countries in which Fascist revolution is already an accomplished fact?

These two aspects of the matter call for separate discussion, though in the end the strands of the argument will need to be united. Let us begin, then, with the more narrowly economic part of the problem. Let us for the moment put all the political complications out of mind—we shall come back to them later—and let us think of the capitalist system purely as an economic system, comparing the crisis of the past few years with previous crises, watching and measuring as far as we can the forces of economic recovery that have made themselves manifest since 1933, and inquiring what is likely to happen to the capitalist system if—to put the matter in the crudest possible way—the capitalist countries do not go to war.

Objection may be taken to this method of considering the question on the ground that the resort to war is so unavoidable an outcome of the present situation of world Capitalism that it is unrealistic to leave it out of account, even at a preliminary stage in the discussion. But it will hardly be denied that the purely economic factors in this situation are of importance, and have a considerable bearing on the likelihood of war; and this in effect is a sufficient reason for endeavouring to form a separate estimate of their character.

We have still, however, to divide our study of this first part of our subject; for it is necessary to give separate consideration to the economic outlook for Capitalism in those countries which are still working under the institutions of capitalist democracy and in those which, while preserving their capitalistic foundations, have passed under the political dictatorship of Fascism. The underlying economic conditions in these two groups of countries are in many respects the same; but at any rate in the short run they exhibit enough differences to need considering apart.

First, then, in the countries of capitalist democracy, where there has been no political revolution, there has been a desperate struggle to re-establish capitalist production after the crisis of 1931 and 1932. In every country, recovery, such as it is, has been achieved only after resort to unorthodox measures. Unorthodoxy has gone to the greatest lengths in the United States, where the prostration of the economic system was most complete. In America, not merely has the almighty dollar sacrificed 40 per cent of its old gold value: the American farmer has been taught how to earn his living by "not raising hogs"; the sacred American Constitution has been exhibited to all men as a banner torn but flying—flying in the face of twentieth-century needs and conditions. President Roosevelt has invoked business confidence with a rain of money, and has been rewarded with an unprecedented majority for his second term, despite the united opposition of bankers and industrialists, who would have preferred, now that he has pulled them out of the slough of despond, to push him well in, and go on their way untroubled by further essays in unorthodox finance. Nevertheless Roosevelt, though big business does not love him for it, has pulled American Capitalism through its more pressing difficulties, and saved it from the sheer collapse which seemed to threaten it only two or three years ago. Immediately, American business is heading towards boom rather than depression, though after the new fashion of Capitalism, even boom nowadays leaves millions of workers unemployed.

In comparison with the United States, Great Britain has held by capitalist orthodoxy, trusting her economic fortunes to the "safe" guidance of the Conservative Party. But even here the economic gale has blown a good many old landmarks away. Free Trade has gone, so completely that not even a Liberal dictatorship could bring it back. The pound sterling headed the flight from the gold standard: the days of gilt-edged 5 per cent seem to be gone for good and all. The exporting industries have lost a great deal of their foreign trade; and the export of British capital has fallen to a fraction of its previous amount. Yet British Capitalism is plainly firm in its saddle; and the British population, except in the depressed areas, have positively benefited by the troubles of the rest of the world because of the cheap imports which even a depreciated pound has been able to purchase in larger quantities than before.

In France, where the orthodoxies were respected longer, Capitalism has been more gravely shaken up. Under stress of the depression, the country came for a moment nearer to Fascism, only to swing over to the left when the Fascist thrust failed actually to overturn the regime. Last of the great capitalist currencies, the *franc* has gone the way of all gold, and turned into the same depreciated paper as the dollar and the pound. Cleaving too long to orthodoxy, because the small *rentiers* knew less than the great capitalists when to swap horses, France has lagged behind in the process of economic recovery. But French Capitalism, though shaken, remains erect; and the possibility that it may meet any serious onslaught upon its stronghold with a Fascist counter-offensive has by no means passed away.

In France, then, the economic issue remains

doubtful; but in both Great Britain and the United States capitalist recovery, on a scale sufficient to avert the immediate threat of breakdown, is already an accomplished fact. The events of the past few years have revealed that in the old-established capitalist countries, and above all in Great Britain, the existing economic system can stand up against a great deal of depression and adversity without positively breaking down. In order to shake Capitalism out of the saddle, or to drive it to political counter-revolution in self-defence, far more powerful shocks are needed even than those under which it has suffered since 1929. That is the plainest lesson for us to draw from the economic crisis which drove Labour out of the Government in Great Britain and brought Roosevelt into it with his "New Deal" in the United States.

Here in Great Britain, we have passed through this tremendous world crisis with our economic institutions practically unchanged. Although British Capitalism was peculiarly vulnerable because of its high degree of dependence on overseas investment and on foreign trade, the crisis here at home has been liquidated—except for the depressed areas—with singularly little disturbance to any of the vital organs of British economic life. It is true that even in the present stage of capitalist recovery a great deal of distress remains unremedied. But that distress is to a great extent now localized, in the so-called "special areas," and affects comparatively little the major part of the population, or even of the working class. Over most of the South, indeed, the sense of crisis was only acute for a few months at most; and actually a majority of the British people, including nearly all those who have been able to keep in regular work, has enjoyed a higher purchasing power during the crisis than ever before. Great Britain, owing to her position as the indispensable import market for some of the principal foodstuffs, has got the full benefit of the enormous fall in agricultural prices; and so great has the effect of this fall been that even the reduced wages paid to the employed workers have enabled them to buy more than they could afford when times were better in the world as a whole.

Moreover, though there has been, of course, a considerable loss of income from overseas investments, it must be admitted that this loss has been very much smaller than anyone would have ventured to predict in face of so serious an upset of the world's economic affairs. On the whole debtors have been quite miraculously eager to pay their debts, or to resume payment as soon as the worst seemed to be over. British Capitalism is still contriving to draw in an astonishingly large amount of tribute from the rest of the world; and some part of this tribute has gone to keeping up the real wages of the employed workers.

The power of British Capitalism to weather the
crisis has thus been greatly strengthened by the
creditor standing of Great Britain in relation to
the outside world. France occupies a similar position,
though to a much smaller extent; and so do the
lesser Capitalisms of Holland and Switzerland. In
the case of countries so situated, and of Great Britain
above all others, the past few years have made it
plain that a good deal more than an economic crisis
—even of such severity as that of 1929 to 1933—
will be needed to shake Capitalism out of the seats
of power, or even to drive it to counter-revolution
as a means of preserving its hold. If we were looking
to purely economic forces to bring about the collapse
of Capitalism in these countries, we should have
still, at the least, to look a long way ahead.

There were, however, in 1929 certain other
capitalist countries possessed of far less reserves
and of far less accumulated economic authority
than Great Britain or France; and among these
countries Germany was of course pre-eminent.
Germany's was a younger Capitalism, and such
reserves as it had once built up had been swept
away as a result of the war. Germany was a debtor
country, on account not only of Reparations but
also of large post-war borrowings for the reconstruction of her economic system. Accordingly, the
crisis found the German economy far more vulnerable than the British or the French; and by 1931

distress among very large sections of the German people had assumed much more formidable dimensions than in either France or Great Britain.

That brings me to my second moral—which is that, when the crisis has developed in such a way as radically to threaten the basic institutions of Capitalism, the outcome has been, not the fall of Capitalism and the substitution for it of a Socialist system, but Fascist revolution. Socialism might, no doubt, have come in Germany, either in the years of crisis immediately after the war, or in the renewed crisis which began in 1929—though by that time the failure to advance towards Socialism during the earlier crisis had largely destroyed its chances, by splitting the working-class movement into wavering factions, when it needed above all else unity against a common enemy. Under the war conditions of 1917 Socialism did succeed in replacing the very weak Capitalism of Czarist Russia, and the attempts at counter-revolution were successfully beaten off. But, as far as we can judge from the experience of the past few years, the impact of an economic crisis severe enough to shake Capitalism to the foundations in a country possessing a developed capitalist structure is less likely to be Socialism than its very antithesis—the reconstruction of Capitalism under the strong hand of a Police State endowed by the capitalists for the explicit purpose of crushing out every form of democratic opinion and organization.

Clearly, if that is the position, we Socialists have to consider very carefully in the light of it what our policy is to be. For it looks very much as if in the older capitalist countries the capitalist system is still strong enough to stand up against the economic forces that are threatening to destroy it, whereas in the countries in which it is not strong enough to defend itself with economic weapons it retains the means of giving itself a new lease of life by bringing Fascism to its aid.

But at this point it seems necessary to turn aside for a moment in order to consider where, in this classification of capitalist countries into the rich *rentier* type and the poor adventurer type, the United States comes in. For America is neither an old-established *rentier* with huge reserves invested abroad nor a mere upstart, which has forged rapidly ahead on a scanty capital, and has nothing to fall back upon when bad times set in. America stands midway between these two types, younger in its experience of Capitalism and more reckless in its methods, but therewith by virtue of its vast agricultural and technical resources and the great size and diversity of its home market very different from Germany, and already in possession of great reserves at home and not inconsiderable investments abroad.

Now, in this as in previous depressions the United States has shown itself far more liable to extreme economic fluctuations than Great Britain, despite

Britain's greater dependence on the rest of the world. This liability to extremes of crisis is mainly the consequence of America's rawness, its lack of balance, of the fact that it has not settled down, as Great Britain has, to a well-established routine. America's institutions, from banks and industries to Government agencies, are far less stable and experienced in meeting difficulties, especially world difficulties, than those of Great Britain. Consequently America had to improvise a vast new organization for dealing with the crisis, and to do this under special hardships imposed by the political system, with its federal constitution and its habitual subservience of political to economic authority. While this improvisation was being prepared, America looked for a time like a country ripe for revolution, except that revolutionary leadership was utterly lacking. But as soon as the new machinery had been set to work, the capitalist organizations began to resume control and to regain confidence in their ability to keep it. There ensued a remarkable recovery—not large enough to cure unemployment or lift production back to the level of 1929, but fully large enough to remove from any reasonable person's mind the belief that the American revolution was near at hand, or that American Capitalism was about to collapse under the impact of purely economic forces.

I believe that anyone who looks fairly and

squarely at the facts will agree that, even if the recovery of the past two or three years gives place to another depression—even to a depression as deep as that from which the world is emerging to-day—it is quite unlikely that, from a purely economic point of view, such a depression will shipwreck either American or British Capitalism.

I have been speaking of "recovery." By this must be understood, of course, recovery in a capitalist sense. From the capitalist point of view both America and Great Britain are now in a highly prosperous condition. But that does not mean that they have solved their social problems, or even succeeded in getting their unemployed back to work. Capitalism can prosper, even while a considerable fraction of the workers starves in idleness. It can prosper, while a considerable fraction of its productive resources rusts unused. It can prosper, and carry as additional social costs the maintenance of those workers for whom it can no longer find any useful work to do. In rich capitalist countries, it can feed the unemployed enough to prevent them from revolting, and still have plenty of profit left over for itself. In poorer countries, where this is harder, it can bring terror and dictatorship to its aid.

As far as Britain and America are concerned, there is nothing to stop their capitalists—nothing *economic*, I mean—from carrying those additional social costs for a long time without collapse. Capitalism will not, of course, meet these costs in a satisfactory human way. It will not give the unemployed or their families a decent life; but it will maintain them, on a low diet, enough to keep them alive, and not enough to give them energy to engage in revolutionary effort. British Capitalism does not need to go Fascist yet awhile. It can manage very much better without Sir Oswald Mosley.

But now let us turn to the situation in the weaker capitalist countries which have resorted to Fascism. Here, the most obvious question that has to be faced is this—Are we to regard Fascism itself as embodying a new economic as well as a new political system, or as merely a mercenary force in the pay of the national capitalists? I cannot rest content with either of these accounts of it. To accept the first is to take the ideological pretensions of the Fascists at their face value, which I am by no means ready to do. But to accept the second view is dangerously to over-simplify.

It is of course manifest that, wherever Fascism has established itself as a political system, the economic power of Capitalism has been maintained and strengthened. In Italy Capitalism is still relatively weak; but it is far stronger than it was before Mussolini seized power. In Germany it is relatively strong; and it is far stronger than it was before Hitler, because the working-class opposition to it has been crushed. In Italy Capitalism is weak enough still for Mussolini to take ideological liberties with it in the name of the Corporative State: in Germany it is no accident, but a direct outcome of the greater strength of Capitalism, that the Nazis have had increasingly to concentrate their nonsense-mongering on racial issues, to let the so-called "Labour Front" sink into complete obscurity, and to keep their hands off Dr. Schacht's purely capitalist manipulations of the German economic machine. There is in Germany not even a pretence that Fascism is establishing the Corporative State.

In Italy, however, as well as in Germany Fascism, in its economic aspect, is no more than Capitalism buttressed by the dictatorial authority of the Police State. Behind the marchings and demonstrations of the Fascist armies and the black- or brown-shirted Fascist militias stand the forces of Capitalism; and, economically, the great capitalists call the tune to which Fascism has to dance. Yet that, true as it is, is not the whole of the truth. For Capitalism, in summoning its Fascist mercenaries to its defence, has conjured up forces which, in political matters, it cannot at all completely control. In order to keep the forces of Socialism under at home, it has to give the nationalist spirit unloosed by Fascism a run for its money in international affairs. It has to keep the minds of the people off home affairs by feeding them continually upon foreign triumphs.

That is why, even when peace would best serve the interests of Capitalism in the Fascist countries, Fascism remains in world affairs a perpetually explosive force. Fascism is not merely a mercenary army with the task of keeping Capitalism in power. It is also politically an independent force, which must seek to maintain its national prestige by scoring continually off other countries.

Capitalism, in the Fascist States, therefore gains an unhampered power of exploiting the workers only at the cost of a certain sacrifice of its independence. In order to fee its mercenaries, it has to accommodate its policies to the Fascist need for national aggrandisement. It cannot seek wealth by buying in the cheapest and selling in the dearest market. It must square its search for profits with the demands of national self-sufficiency with a view to war. It must regard primarily the home market, even though the home market is necessarily depressed as a result of the beating down of wages and standards of living—a logical consequence of the destruction of Trade Unions and other institutions of democratic defence. That is why, in the Fascist countries, huge expenditure on armaments appears not as waste of the productive resources, but as an indispensable means of employing them; for how else is production to find an outlet when standards of living have been artificially depressed in the profit-makers' interest? The State becomes the principal consumer; and the State, driven by the inner contradictions of the system towards a militant policy of expansion and conquest, arms for war.

I cannot convey further this characterisation of Fascist Capitalism without bringing in explicitly the factors which I began by setting temporarily aside—the politico-economic, as distinct from the purely economic, factors making for the survival or supersession of the capitalist system. But, before we come to consider these factors directly, let us ask whether there is any greater prospect of Capitalism collapsing, under the impact of purely economic forces, in the Fascist countries than in, say, Great Britain or the United States.

It is often suggested that there is. We are told about the immense economic difficulties under which Germany and Italy are labouring to-day. Many people hoped that these difficulties would be formidable enough for even a half-hearted League blockade to prevent Italy from conquering Abyssinia; and many people even to-day hold out the hope that the German economy may collapse of itself under the weight imposed upon it by military expenditure and the pursuit of economic self-sufficiency under the Nazi "Plan."

I believe this view to be totally wrong. No doubt the economic situation in both Germany and Italy is very difficult. No doubt, in Germany, Dr. Schacht is under the continuous necessity of performing most remarkable feats of jugglery in order to keep the balls in the air. But even if Dr. Schacht were to drop the balls, that would not mean the collapse of Capitalism or of the Hitler regime. It would not mean, even if Germany passed through a still more grinding crisis than any that has befallen her as yet, that there would be a German revolution or the substitution for German Capitalism of an alternative economic system. The Nazis have no alternative; and there is no force now left in Germany capable of making a revolution—as long as Germany remains at peace.

It is, of course, easy enough for the economic theorist to demonstrate that the Economic Nationalism, which is the economic aspect of Fascist Capitalism, is wasting opportunities for the advancement of wealth. Is it not largely forfeiting the manifest advantages of the international division of labour, producing things dearly when it could buy them cheap, and thereby necessarily impoverishing the people and the nation? To be sure it is. But we must compare the working of Fascist Capitalism not with the ideal economic society postulated by the economic theorists as a norm, but with the actual conditions in the countries of non-Fascist Capitalism. Now, in such countries as Great Britain and the United States, it is true that more advantage is taken—in spite of Mr. Elliot and

his Marketing Boards—of the international division
of labour. In fact, to us in Great Britain great
advantage has accrued from it during the past few
years. The non-Fascist countries are not incurring
the same types of waste and impoverishment as are
being incurred by both Germany and Italy, or at
any rate are not incurring them to anything like
the same extent. But the non-Fascist countries are
incurring plenty of other kinds of waste—above
all, the waste involved in leaving a large part of
their productive resources unemployed. When the
Fascist dictators are confronted with a mass of
unused labour they do on the whole set that labour
to work, even if they do not employ it in the most
economic ways; whereas the non-Fascist countries
for the most part let it rot away in idleness.

Which of these systems results in the greater
economic loss I do not pretend to say. Very likely
it is about six of one and half a dozen of the other.
The one casts aside most of the advantages of the
international division of labour: the other condemns
millions of its citizens to bare and useless existence
on the dole. They are both profoundly wasteful and
uneconomic; but there is no such clear balance of
disadvantage against the Fascists as even entitle
us to predict confidently that their system will
collapse, while the other survives.

I think, then, it is quite a mistake to suppose that,
by contrast with "democratic" Capitalism, Fascist

Capitalism will break down because of its inability to feed the people. It will not feed them well; but it will feed them somehow—at least enough to avert positive collapse.

It is of course true that when Fascism suppresses the working-class movement and destroys the organized forces which exist to defend the "bottom dog," it tips the distribution of wealth in favour of the rich and against the poor, and tends to depress the entire wealth of the community. But Fascism is not without means of offsetting that disadvantage so as to prevent it from engendering a revolutionary attitude. In Great Britain—and the position is much the same in America—the most glaring contrasts exist between the working-class standards of living in different parts of the country—say, between South Wales, Durham and Clydeside on the one hand and the developing industrial and commercial areas in the South of England on the other. There is flagrant maldistribution of incomes among the poor themselves, as well as between the poor and the rich. Now Fascism, I believe, creates even greater injustices in distribution as between rich and poor; but it distributes better as between one poor man and another. Unhampered by such bodies as Trade Unions, it is better able to make the poor man who is a little better off maintain the poor man who is a little worse off, without making any call upon the rich. That power to make the poor share out among themselves is, I believe, an extraordinarily effective safeguard against revolution in the Fascist countries, and an additional reason why the wastes involved in Fascist economic policy cannot be expected in the near future to cause economic collapse.

Therefore I maintain that, despite the growing contradictions of Capitalism—the increasing contrast between the power to create and the power to distribute wealth—the collapse of the system is not imminent, from purely economic causes, in either the Fascist or the non-Fascist countries. If Capitalism is in truth near its end, it will be brought down not directly by internal economic collapse, but by war. War will be needed to cause in the near future so great a collapse as to lead to revolution or the enforced reconstruction of the economic system on a non-capitalist basis. If Capitalism cannot survive for some considerable time yet, that will be because it cannot keep the peace.

Clearly, if the matter were in the hands of our British capitalists, the peace would be kept. For British Capitalism, unless it is positively attacked, has no interest in going to war. It has so much already that it would be insane to take risks in order to gain more. So clearly is this the view of British Capitalism that already a Government with strong imperialist leanings has sacrificed all its principles and one end of the Mediterranean, and shown its willingness to sacrifice the other end, rather than run even a slight risk of a war in which it might have found itself allied with the Soviet Union against the Fascist Powers. I verily believe it would give away the entire Empire, province by province, rather than find itself so embroiled. No other supposition can explain the trends of British foreign policy during the past year.

Now, I cannot say that British Capitalism is wrong, in its own interests, in taking up this attitude. It would, I believe, invoke at need British Fascism to save it from British Socialism; and internationally I am not surprised to find that it greatly prefers Hitler and Mussolini to Stalin and Largo Caballero, or even to Léon Blum. Democracy is, for Capitalism, merely an expedient, whereas property is a sacred principle. Better lose the Empire, and defend Capitalism in Great Britain, than run the risk of using the imperial forces on the Socialist side in the world struggle between Fascism and Socialism.

At any rate, that is how British Capitalism has behaved, and is behaving to-day. That means that it does not want war; and that gives it, for the time being, a strong hold over the British people, who do not want war either.

There are, however, other capitalist countries which, whether or not they actually want war, stand in need of continual victories of prestige among their own peoples, and are prepared to face war rather than suffer any setback which would seriously damage their prestige. These countries, as we have seen, are driven by the exigencies of their internal situation to press continually outwards, and after such "victory" to keep on demanding more. Even if they do not want war, they do want a world in which they can keep on exacting concessions by the threat of war. It follows that they must prepare for war, and be ready to embark upon it if at any time the countries at whom they are thrusting, goaded beyond enthusiasm, determine to make a stand.

If Fascism were simply a mercenary in the pay of Capitalism, and bound on all occasions to obey the crack of the capitalist whip, this situation would not exist. At any rate for some time to come, German Capitalism and Italian Capitalism would come to terms with British and French Capitalism, sooner than declare war upon them. But in fact Fascism, though it could never have come to power in either Italy or Germany without the aid of the great capitalists who financed its operations, has become politically an independent force capable of moulding the short-run course of events. Fascism can make war even against the judgment of the capitalists; and the capitalists must allow it in the last resort to make war rather than lose prestige because they cannot dispense with it as an instrument for preserving their economic power. In short, world Capitalism, in calling Fascism to its defence, has raised up devils whose day-to-day bedevilments it is now unable to control. Economically, Capitalism controls Fascist policy, in the sense of keeping it firmly to the protection of capitalist property. But politically it does not. Doubtless, if the Fascist States waged a great European war, and won it, Capitalism would dictate the settlement, just as it dictated the settlement of 1919. But Fascist Capitalism cannot stop the Fascist countries from menacing the world with war. Nor in the last resort would it wish to; for Capitalism would greatly prefer world war to the world victory of Socialism.

In this political independence of Fascism lies the chief immediate danger. World Capitalism, left to itself, would for the present prefer to keep the peace. Fascism, on the other hand, cannot afford to wait; for waiting wrecks its prestige. It lives on conjuring up enemies: as soon as it is opposed, it must smash its way to victory, or lose face. Verily Capitalism has called up devils to put down its enemies; and its devils threaten to tear civilisation to pieces.

But where, in all this, do the constructive forces of Socialism come in? They are still alive, and free to act, in the non-Fascist countries; and in some —in Sweden and Denmark, for example, and latterly in France—they have been doing excellent work in combating the economic crisis and extending the power of the parliamentary State over the regulation of capitalist institutions. Can they not, here and elsewhere, where parliamentary institutions survive, go further than this, and begin speedily upon the constructive task of replacing Capitalism by a Socialist system that will unloose the powers of production and institute a new age of plenty on a basis of modern technique?

What—since that comes nearest home to most of us—can the forces of constructive Socialism do, here and now, in Great Britain? To that question I want to devote the last part of this essay; and I fear I must begin with a few uncomforting words about the Labour Party's political prospects and the probable government of this country in the immediate future.

I have to say quite categorically that there does not seem to me to be any probability, as far as the foreseeable forces are concerned, of a clear Labour majority either at the next General Election or at the next after that. In order to win a majority, Labour would have to win nearly every seat at present held by the Government by a margin of less than 6,000 votes, and to do this without losing more than a very few of the seats which it now holds. Unless the political situation changes in quite unpredictable ways, this seems to me to be simply out of the question. I can see the Labour Party gaining a considerable number of additional seats; but I cannot, by any stretch of the imagination, see it winning an independent majority along its present lines. Nor can I see much prospect even of a return to the situation of 1929, when Labour and Independent Liberalism commanded between them a majority in the House of Commons; for Liberalism has split since then, and there are no signs of a Liberal revival on any significant scale.

If this view is correct, it confronts us Socialists with an outlook that must give us very serious food for thought. During the past year we have been an impotent political minority, looking on while the Government has betrayed in turn, every principle that was supposed to be guiding British policy— while it has destroyed the League of Nations, handed the Mediterranean over to Mussolini and the Far East to Japan, compelled France to desert the Spanish democracy by threatening M. Blum with the rupture of the Locarno Treaties, in short in every possible way encouraged the Fascist aggressors to believe that they have only to threaten war in order to be allowed to take whatever they covet. By these successive betrayals the hope of building up a League system of pooled security has been wantonly thrown away. The danger of world war has been made infinitely greater and more immediate: the prospect that the entire civilisation of Western Europe may be eclipsed has been infinitely increased.

Yet, if we are to wait until Labour gets its coveted

majority, what escape from this humiliation can we look for within the next ten years? Ten years! When within ten months Fascism will certainly have committed as many more acts of wanton aggression: when within ten months all Europe may be engulfed in war!

Within far less than ten years the entire situation in Europe will almost certainly have so changed that nothing that can be said now will have any relevance. Yet the leaders of Labour are apparently prepared to spend the next ten years fishing in troubled waters for a majority that may not be there.

I do not feel like condemning myself, and I hope my fellow-countrymen do not feel like condemning themselves, to ten years of political impotence— ten years that will be decisive for the entire future of Socialism and of Western civilisation. If the diagnosis that I have been putting forward is anything like correct, our policy needs radical re-adjustment: it simply cannot be right as it is. This readjustment, I believe, has two aspects, the domestic and the international, and in both the issues that are at stake are fundamentally the same.

It will be agreed that, from the standpoint of Socialism or democracy or ordinary human decency, the record of the past year is one of humiliating defeat. It is a record of the undermining, by one thing after another, of the forces which are capable of moulding the future of human society without war—of moulding it, hopefully and step by step, into the shapes which are indispensable if Western civilisation is to survive at all. It is a record of one surrender after another, one strengthening after another of the forces that are most dangerous to democracy and peace, one discouragement after another to those men and nations that are seeking to play their parts in building up a saner world. As long as these trends continue—and that means as long as a Government of the Right remains in power—the democratic forces will be more and more weakened and discouraged, and less and less able or inclined to make common cause for the defence of civilisation. There will be more and more defections to the Fascist side, more and more frightened proclamations of neutrality, more and more so-called "civil wars" which are in reality class-wars of international Fascism against democracy. We can see what that means in Spain to-day; and we can see there with what ruthless brutality the Fascists wage their wars. The longer we stand aside, the more the forces of democracy are weakened and demoralised; and the more the world comes to believe that treaty-breaking and savage cruelty are the things that pay.

What is the cause for this lamentable disunity among the forces of democracy and human decency? It is, of course, that in every capitalist country the capitalists in the mass, though they may still repudiate Fascism, greatly prefer it to any sort of Socialism. They are determined above all else to keep their wealth; and, while they do not want Fascism where they can govern without it, they will do nothing that might strengthen Socialism against it in the world as a whole. As long as a capitalist Government governs Great Britain, it will be impossible for Great Britain to range itself internationally with any grouping that stands for united opposition to the Fascist aggressors. For such a grouping must include the Socialists, and indeed depend upon them for leadership and direction. British Capitalism will have none of such an alliance, within or without the League of Nations. It prefers Hitler and Mussolini to a democracy which is based upon the Left.

If then we want to achieve international unity against the Fascist threat of war, we must turn out our capitalist Government, and put in its place a Government of the Left. But for that we cannot afford to wait ten years, or even half as long. Unless we are prepared to see the world laid in ruins by war, and Fascism triumphant all over Europe, we must pull this British Government down. For Britain, by virtue of her power, holds the key to the entire balance of forces in Europe.

That means that, here in Great Britain, our immediate task is not the getting of Socialism—for that is not within our grasp—but the achievement of a sufficient combination of Left forces to swing this country into an international democratic alliance for the preservation of peace. It means getting Great Britain into a system of real pooled security, with France and Russia and every lesser Power that is prepared to play its part. It means creating an international compact so strong that even predatory Fascism will not dare to challenge its might.

Now that involves a broader combination at home than it is possible to achieve under the Labour Party alone. It means a broader combination than can be achieved by merely persuading Labour and Liberalism to act together. It means a People's Front broad enough to embrace a great many people who, largely out of mistrust for the competence of the Labour and Liberal Parties, have hitherto voted for the Government candidates. It involves therewith a broad appeal to the generous spirit of youth—an appeal to principles, and not merely to temporary expediencies, vital as these are.

Such a notion, of course, from the standpoint of devoted party adherents, involves a very big wrench. Take, for example, our Labour Party statesmen. For years they have been looking forward to winning a clear majority for their party. They have been prophesying that Liberalism would in due course melt away to nothing, while they stood under it with a bucket and caught the drops. Well, Liberalism's melting point has been low enough; but the Labour man's bucket seems to have had a hole in it, for somehow the votes lost to Liberalism seem mostly to have gone, not to Labour, but to the capitalist side. It is surely high time for the Labour Party to realise that merely to wait upon the dissolution of Liberalism, in the expectation that a Labour majority will thereupon automatically accrue, is a fool's game. If that is our attitude, we are living in a fool's paradise.

For that is not what will happen. Even apart from the danger that war will be on us long before the Liberal lump has wholly melted away, we shall in fact win over to Socialism the dissolving elements of the old system only in as far as we are able to constitute ourselves the leaders of a national and international crusade with a plain purpose that all can understand. We must make a crusade that will appeal not only to Trade Unionists, and to old Socialists, but also, because of the direct relevance to the immediate issues of to-day and to-morrow, to the great majority of ordinary decent people, whatever their past political affiliations may have been.

To-day, it is futile to build our immediate policy on our hopes of the Socialist Commonwealth. What we have to do now is to secure the foundations on which we can hope to build at all. For our chance of building Socialism in the future depends on our success now in saving Western civilisation from entire eclipse.

This conviction has been behind everything that I have written. I do not believe, as some Socialists apparently do still believe, that Socialism is inevitable. I do not believe that there is over Great Britain, or over Western Europe, some almighty watching power which has ordained that, however feebly and foolishly we behave, Socialism is bound to come. I do believe that Socialism is the logical sequel to Capitalism, and that only on Socialist foundations can our civilisation escape its contradictions, or continue to advance, or indeed avoid sheer dissolution before long. But why should it progress, unless we make it? Why should it not decay and dissolve, as other civilisations have perished before in the world's history? Man makes his history, for good or ill: it is not made for him. He makes it, indeed, within environing economic conditions to which he must conform; and the penalty for failure to conform to these conditions is defeat. But defeat is fully as possible as victory. It depends on us whether we succeed or fail.

I see then as the alternative to Socialism nothing but decay. Economically Capitalism could hang on for a long time yet, if the economic forces were left to work themselves out alone. But it would be a decaying Capitalism, more and more in conflict with the advancing technical forces of production, less and less able to employ the people, or to distribute the goods and services which it would be technically competent to produce. But, even if there were no wars to disturb the even tenor of its decline, every slide downward would make it harder to build up Socialism in a sane and constructive way, and make it likelier that Socialism could come, if at all, only painfully and slowly out of the welter of destitution and inefficiency which dying Capitalism would leave behind.

But I do not think that is how things will happen. Capitalism will not wither slowly away. What is far more probable, unless we make quickly our national and international stand, is war—war to the death, international civil war bloodier and more desperate than any conflict in the world's history— war that is likely to leave behind it the sheer wreck of everything that is valuable in this civilisation in which we live.

That is not inevitable either—any more than Socialism is inevitable. We have still time to prevent it, if we can pluck up our fainting courage and reassemble our scattered wits to the task. We want to build Socialism, I hope, not amid the ruins of a broken civilisation, but on the foundations that have been laid for us by centuries of man's successful struggle to master the forces of nature and the arts of civilised living. We want to build up Socialism in that way because it will be better built, and

46

because we value human happiness, and shrink back appalled at the prospect of human misery which the alternative involves.

That is a reason, as I see it, for acting promptly to widen our democratic front, not at any sacrifice of our Socialist principles, but by concentrating for the moment upon those things which we can hope practically to achieve, and above all on those immediate measures which are essential for salvaging civilisation in the present crisis. Pooled security for the preservation of peace; mutual resistance to Fascist aggression; the defence of democratic institutions at home and abroad; and therewith a short, simple, practical programme of domestic reorganisation and reform, based on the re-employment of the workless and the immediate raising of the minimum standard of life. These, I believe, are the ingredients of a policy capable of rallying the united enthusiasm of the Left. But unless we act speedily, in the spirit of democratic unity against the devilish forces that have been let loose on the world, I fear greatly that we may act too late.

2

ECONOMIC NATIONALISM: CAN IT CONTINUE?

Sir Arthur Salter, K.C.B.

SOME years ago, Mr. Wedgwood Benn,[1] you came to Geneva, when I was in charge of the League of Nations' economic and financial work. I recall that time with a painful sense of contrast. We then seemed in a new dawn after the devastating chaos of the War. A small band of us at Geneva were taking a part—it seemed then a not inconsiderable part—in helping to rebuild the foundations of the world economic and financial system shattered by those four years. It is, perhaps, one of the happiest fates that man can have, to take part in a great constructive effort of that kind, difficult enough to be interesting, promising enough to be encouraging. We thought we were rebuilding the world and, for a long time, we had reason to think so. Now, as we survey the present scene, most—though happily not all—of what we built lies in ruins before us. We have faced since then, in 1929 the economic depression, in 1931 the financial crisis, in 1933 the

[1] The chairman at the lecture.

48

change in Germany with its far-reaching consequences, of which the tale is not yet complete.

The particular task in which I was engaged when
you came to Geneva, Mr. Chairman, was one that
is very relevant to the theme of this evening. It was
that of trying to remove the impediments to international trade and helping to construct the financial
and economic framework within which it could
again resume its place in the world. To some extent,
my discussion to-night will take the form of imagining
myself back again at my old job, and trying once
more, in the changed circumstances, to help to
create the conditions under which world trade can
again revive, and considering how far I would now
advise a change in the strategy and the tactics
which we then adopted.

First of all, however, let me say just a few words
as to what I understand by economic nationalism.
I will not spend time in going over the familiar
argument as to Free Trade and Protection. Whether
we like it or not, we must at this period certainly
seek a method of extending international trade
which is not simply that of trying to knock down
tariffs whenever we see them. In some way or other
we have to evolve a new system which is compatible with many developments which we may or
may not regret, but in the modern world are now
irrevocable. We must, I think, assume the continuance
of State intervention in economic enterprise, and of

D   49

protective duties as one of its methods. And we must find a method of encouraging world trade that is consistent with this system. That it is desirable to increase international trade and to get rid of the worst forms of economic nationalism, I need hardly argue. If you want a simple illustration of protection carried to its logical conclusion, I would ask you to think of the time when we were blockading Germany with our cruisers and Germany was blockading us with her submarines. Militarily speaking, the submarines were an instrument of attack against us, the British cruisers were an instrument of attack against Germany; but, economically speaking, the submarine was giving us economic protection, our cruisers were giving Germany economic protection in a very effective and complete form. What did the submarine do? It made it extremely difficult and expensive for foreign imports to come in. It raised prices and gave that margin of protected prosperity upon which, we are told, industry must depend. It raised a shelter behind which our industrial activity could develop to the fullest advantage. What the submarine did for us in that happy fashion, the British cruiser did for Germany in an even more complete fashion. That is economic protection carried to its logical conclusion.

I do not need to argue that economic nationalism in its present form is at once an enormous impediment to economic recovery here and throughout the world.

It is also, however, one of the most powerful forces which add to the dangers of war. It is from the second point of view, seeing that the menace of war is probably predominant in our minds to-day, that I propose mainly to discuss the question.

Speaking from this point of view, I want immediately to make what I think is an important distinction. Economically autarchy involves loss, and the less we have of it the better. But, from the point of view of world peace, there is another kind of economic nationalism which is more permanently and more disproportionately provocative and dangerous than autarchy; that is the form of economic nationalism which consists in the intervention of States, with all the power of a national government and the armed forces behind it, in the competitive scramble for foreign trade. There is a very great deal of difference, from the point of view of provocation, of creating a sense of injustice and a situation against which other countries will react, between this and merely preserving your own markets for your own industries. The latter involves loss and also causes friction, when it is suddenly imposed, but it is not in itself so provocative because each country recognizes the right of other countries to manage their own national markets as they like. It is realized that, in the last resort, wisely or unwisely, every country has a right to keep its own markets for its own industrialists. What is very much more dangerous as a long-term factor in the world situation is the use of the instrument of the State for the purpose of assisting and taking part in the competition for foreign markets, for the neutral trade of the world, which is no more one country's possession than another's. With foreign markets, from this point of view, I must include colonial markets, for, rightly or wrongly, non-colonial Powers do not regard Great Britain as having the same unconditional and unrestricted rights over a dependent tropical country as over the County of Kent or the County of Middlesex. Therefore, from the point of view of peace as a long-term factor, the economic nationalism which consists in intervention by the State in foreign trade, whether in the form of subsidies for exports, or of a diplomat's representations designed to assist the competition of an individual exporter with the prestige of his Government, or of the manipulation of currency in order to get a competitive advantage from currency depreciation, is important as a political factor altogether out of proportion to its actual economic effect.

Now, I think there is no doubt whatever that economic nationalism in both forms, but particularly in this second form, is a very large factor indeed in the present international situation and among the causes that are creating a danger of war. I say that from actual observation of the present international system and not on any kind of *a priori* ground. I am not, in fact, an economic determinist. I thoroughly distrust explanations of the course of world history that are over-simplified and that explain things in terms of one only of the factors or one only of the constituents of the human mind and character. I have the greatest distrust of people who say that when the Greeks attacked Troy, although they thought they were avenging the rape of Helen, they were really seeking a trade route to the Black Sea. It is true that, throughout history, the political and economic are entwined. It is equally true, if we go behind the analysis of events and look into the psychology of man of which all human events and all human institutions are the expression, we find an economic motive. We find hunger. But we find not only hunger. We find also pugnacity. We find that kind of local pride which is the source of racial passion, and becomes intertwined with economic motives. I think it is a mistake to select a single one of these strands of a complex web and say this is the one on which all the others depend. And if we seek the causes of war in other centuries or in recent history, I do not think it is at all true to say that in any real sense economic forces are the only or even the principal factors. I do not believe, for example, that it is at all a realistic view of the international situation before 1914 to say that the real forces making for war were then the economic factors. They were, I believe, both remote and subordinate.

If all the economic causes of friction that you could possibly hope to have removed had been eliminated, you would not have substantially changed the situation. I agree entirely with the statement to that effect that Mr. Spender makes in his recent history of the last fifty years. I do not think any observer, looking closely at the actual situation and not misled by any *a priori* theory, would doubt that the real cause of the war of 1914, if we are talking of general causes, was the international anarchy, the fact that there was no system in the world which could do for those questions which transcend national frontiers what a national government does within the limits of the State. In the absence of any such system, even trivial objects of dispute or differences of policy, having no other means of settlement, may lead to war.

If you look at the actual occasions of dispute, they seem fantastically trivial in comparison with the terrific instrument of war that was ultimately used to resolve them. In the series of events that preceded 1914 the prize of success in diplomacy was usually not the specific economic or territorial question in dispute; it was success itself. What each country aimed at was increased prestige or the avoidance of any loss of prestige. For prestige was the only means of securing any objective of policy without war, and to prevail once was to make a later success, in attempting any other objective of policy, more likely. Therefore, if we were dealing now with the period 1910, 1911, 1912 and 1913, I should not be stressing economic nationalism, as I am now, as one of the major factors in the international situation. But now in this present situation, I think beyond any kind of question it is. We have been trying since the War to replace international anarchy by international government in the form of the League of Nations. We seemed to be succeeding, but for some time now that attempt has been—not, I hope, irrevocably— failing, because the forces that it encountered were too great; and, beyond any question, economic factors were among the principal of those forces.

Why have economic factors become so very much more important now than they were in the pre-1914 situation? Above all, I think for one reason, that we have passed from a world that was predominantly a world of *laissez-faire* to a world that is predominantly one of State intervention. The great difference when this change takes place is that, not only are many of the safety valves of the old system removed, but the quarrels and frictions and disputes that inevitably arise from all the multitudinous efforts and competition of men in all countries, are converted from being quarrels of individuals to being the quarrels of States. In proportion as that happens, economic disputes become a dangerous factor in the international situation. You may think that, in saying that, I am arguing against Socialism. I am not, because the main issue, in my view, is now not whether you should have *laissez-faire* or Socialism. *Laissez-faire* has gone in any case. The important issue in the modern world is whether we shall have some form of State system which secures that the State is the instrument and the servant of the public or whether the State, which will certainly intervene in the economic life of the world increasingly and over a vast scale, shall be the servant not of the public but of organized economic interests. Now, from the point of international peace, apart from any other consideration, there is one thing which is much more dangerous than responsible negotiations between States on matters of possible friction. That is the irresponsible pressure of powerful organized economic groups (which themselves only require to look at their immediate economic interests) upon a State which, so to speak, abdicates its responsibility and allows itself to be used as the instrument of pressure in competition with other countries for the general foreign trade of the world. This is the development that has taken place on a large scale and causes economic nationalism to be a factor in the peace of the world of much greater importance than in the pre-1914 world.

Not, of course, that economic forces are now the only ones; I am not even going to say that they are more important than all political and racial passions. They cannot indeed be exactly weighed against each other. Let us first consider the nature of any form of international government that is being constructed, and then the character of the forces which it will need to control. These are on the one hand economic, and on the other, racial and political. We cannot, however, assess these separately and then, by adding the two results, estimate their total strength. That is not the true relationship of economic and political factors. Many people seem to be under the extraordinary delusion, Mr. Chairman, that two and two always make four. It is perfectly true of concrete and inanimate objects. But it is not at all true of living forces. If you add one chemical substance to another the resulting amalgam may have either a terrific explosive force, that is altogether out of proportion to the sum of their separate strengths—or it may have none at all.

This is the analogy we should have in mind when considering the interaction of the economic and political forces. Let me give you an example. We have recently had the affair of Abyssinia. Now if there had never been a League of Nations at all, British militancy, challenged with what was happening in Abyssinia, would have shown itself, I think, to have a very considerable strength and force. If, on the other hand, there had been no question of British militancy and you had only League militancy, this might have meant something. But when you added the one force to the other, what was the result?

As nearly as no matter, nothing at all. That is an example of one result. Now consider the opposite result, illustrated from the same event. There was a certain amount of what one may call political passions, ambitions and desires in Italy—all that constitutes to our mind Italian nationalism—the desire for glory, the desire to paint something red, or green, or whatever it is Italians paint a colonized area—all the motives except economic ones. If there had been all these, but nothing of any possible economic value in Abyssinia, the political passions might have flared up and flared out. But in fact there was *some* economic treasure in Abyssinia. At the same time it was incredibly small compared with the cost involved in getting it, something of which you could hardly conceive any ruler of a State saying: "It is worth my while in order to get that to go to the expense of sending an expedition of 250,000 men down into the tropics." But when these two things were added together the result was a force making for war terrifically greater than the sum of the two constituent elements. The real economic advantage of possessing a country with such limited opportunities for colonization that in twenty years it would be impossible to settle a number of colonists equal to the increase in Italian population every six months, is minute. But when this minute advantage is combined with nationalist passions it becomes indefinitely magnified. A waste of bare rocks and desert becomes an Eldorado of riches and a land of promise for all the surplus and impoverished population of Italy. The result is a national passion strong enough to launch a large expedition of which we shall see the grievous consequences for many a day to come.

I come back to my original and surely obvious statement, that it is of the utmost importance that we should attempt to eliminate economic nationalism in its present form in the interests alike of peace and of prosperity. Somehow or other we must attempt to construct a system under which international trade can be again resumed. Yes, but how are we to do it? At this point I must make what you may think is somewhat of a digression. For, in order to explain precisely why I think that the method that we attempted before, in 1927 and onwards, for the enlargement of international trade now requires to be changed, I must place it in its proper perspective as a part of the whole of the first post-War reconstruction effort. Only thus shall we see the different task that now confronts us when we embark on the second great reconstructive effort: to rebuild a world shattered, not by a recent war, but by an economic depression and a financial crisis. I want to explain, if I can, what was the real character of that first effort of reconstruction, what was the real cause and explanation of the apparent failure.

Doubtless there are many of you who look back

over the efforts of the last eighteen years to reconstruct a tolerable world system, as if it were a
record of perpetual defeat, a tragedy of unrelieved
failure. That would be, in my view, a comple mis-
reading. The tragedy was in some respects greater;
it was a tragedy of success, of great success, in
reconstructing a system which, almost as soon as we
had successfully reconstructed it, was found to be on
foundations not strong enough to bear it, was found
to be not strong enough to contend with and control
the new conditions generated by the War, was found
to be in some respects unsuitable for the conditions
of the modern world.

Let me recall to you what it was that we tried to
do from 1919 onwards, particularly that little band
of people who had been concerned with economic
control during the War and, with their principal,
although not their only, centre in Geneva, attempted
to reconstruct the system which the War had shattered.
After the conclusion of four years of destructive
war the magnitude of that chaos, confusion, and
dislocation was such that the War seemed a
sufficient explanation of almost all the evils from
which we were suffering. Looking back over those
four years, the world of 1913, for most of us—
certainly most of those in directing or controlling
positions, whether as officials or ministers—seemed
in retrospect, whatever its defects at the time, a
kind of Paradise, from which for four years we had

been shut out by the flaming sword of destruction. It seemed a sufficient goal for all our efforts to return to the Paradise from which we had been temporarily excluded. Therefore all over the world, in almost every country, though not all, you found that the goal of every minister, every official, the leaders of movements in every country, was to get back to the pre-War system. As we looked around, we saw first the material destruction of war, we saw that capital renewal had been neglected for four years, railways, roads and so on had deteriorated. We said, "Let us repair that destruction. Let us renew that capital." We recalled next what, in retrospect, seemed that miraculous system of competitive price regulation by which all the multitudinous processes of man's life found their adjustments with each other and we saw this system had been impeded by all kinds and forms of State intervention and control. And though I must, in justice to my colleagues and myself, say that some of us put in a warning and said, "Do not destroy these controls too quickly," most people said, "The thing to be done is to get rid of all these impediments at once and restore a system under which the old automatic adjustments can again become effective." We looked then at the currency system of the world; under one stress and another it had left its sheet-anchor of gold and turned to paper, and we saw the terrible consequences. Even in our country the effects were serious, while in some countries, like Germany, prices went to a point at which the whole basis of interchange of goods was destroyed and there was complete social and economic chaos. Well, then, we said, let us get back to the position in which gold can again occupy its throne; we devoted our efforts to restoring gold as the currency of the world. So, too, when we saw that the volume of international trade had been reduced by new trade impediments, we said, wherever we saw a tariff or other trade impediment, let us try and get it removed. We saw that the whole financial system of the world had been strained by reparations and by war debts, and that, with these burdens upon it, it was unable to secure the ordinary flow of capital from one country to another. Very well, we said, let us try and settle those debts at a reasonable figure. We saw, further, that apart from those general difficulties, certain countries had been subjected to strains of quite exceptional severity, and were broken and unable to keep step with other countries in the return to recovery—Austria, Hungary, Bulgaria, Greece and one or two others. Very well, we said, in addition to our general policy we must have special international action to restore those countries. That was our programme; it was the restoration of the pre-War system, with only one notable addition—that of the construction of a tentative form of international government, the League of Nations. Except for that addition to the diplomatic systems of the different countries, the aim of the first reconstruction effort after the War was to restore the pre-War system. And we did not fail; we succeeded.

Let me recall to you the position ten years after the War. In 1928 prosperity had passed pre-War standards in almost every country in the world. There was indeed rather more unemployment, but in most countries it was not very serious, and where it was serious, as here, the general prosperity enabled the unemployed to be maintained in a position of comfort equal to that of the full-time unskilled worker not so very long before. International trade had not fully recovered its volume and value, but any difference in pre-War standard was more than compensated by the expansion of home markets. Currencies almost all over the world had been restored again to the sheet-anchor of gold. Some success was reached even in reducing tariffs in 1927 and 1928, and it looked as if considerable further progress might soon be made. All the broken countries of central and south-eastern Europe had been restored and brought to a level with other countries of a similar type. In Austria and Hungary we had found chaos and had restored a reasonable measure of prosperity. In Greece and Bulgaria we had successfully established whole populations of refugees on the land. And last of all the new instrument of international government, the League of Nations, seemed to be successfully achieving its task. In addition to the great countries that were members from the first, Germany had joined, and it seemed clear that Russia would soon join also. America was still outside, but was co-operating increasingly, so that it seemed likely that in a few years Covenant and Kellogg Pact together would constitute a comprehensive peace system. The Central European problem, that of relations between Germany and France, seemed almost solved. The great improvement in the relations between those two countries was expressed by the Locarno Treaties of 1925. Considerable progress had been made with naval disarmament and the way seemed clear for progress in land disarmament as well. Parliamentary systems, with the one notable exception of Italy, had been maintained. In Austria, Hungary, Czechoslovakia, and Poland—which had little or no experience of true Parliamentary government—the Parliamentary system had been extended.

Ten years after the War, then, prosperity had been restored. Peace, with Locarno, the Kellogg Pact and close association with America, seemed reasonably assured. We had only to go a little longer along the same path, while each country proceeded to solve its domestic and social problems at home, and the world seemed to have a reasonable prospect of a civilization scarcely less stable, certainly much richer, than anything that had been known in the world previously. That was in 1928. We had restored the world system, the old pre-War system, and for the moment it seemed sufficient. And then in 1929 came the economic depression; then, in 1931, what was much more important than the economic depression, the collapse of the whole monetary and financial system of the world, taking the world depression to unprecedented depths; then in 1933 the beginning of the destruction on a large scale of the free institutions of the world, with all the repercussions that have followed in subsequent years; then in 1934–35 the weakening of the new hope of the world—the League of Nations. And so we arrive at where we are now. That, as I say, was a tragedy, not just of failure, but of success in building a system which as soon as it was built showed itself to be on foundations not strong enough, to be too weak to control the new forces generated by the War, and in some respects to be unsuitable for the conditions of the modern world.

What are those conditions of the modern world that are so different, that made this old pre-War system thus re-established unsuitable for its task? There are the two main changes, one of which I have already referred to. In the first place, organized economic forces are immensely stronger than in the last-century world. Secondly we no longer have, in a world of *laissez-faire*, competition between individuals and small units. We have large, organized economic

E   65

forces, and State control and State intervention, of one kind or another, in practically every country in the world. With those two new factors the old system of finance and currency, developed as a counterpart of *laissez-faire* both in domestic economy and in external trade, proved to be not strong enough to control the new forces.

Let me give you one illustration of the way in which new economic forces proved too strong for the old currency system. You remember what happened here in 1925. We came back on to the old parity of 4·86 to the £. At that time this parity was an over-valuation of the £. It meant that, with the £ suddenly brought back with a jerk to 10 per cent above its real value at the time, it was necessary, if British export trade was to remain on a competitive level, that prices should be reduced. Well, in the old world, prices would have been reduced, we should have gone through the process of deflation, wages would have gone down, costs would have gone down, and we should have maintained our foreign trade. But prices refused to go down, because in the modern world, as compared with the pre-War world, the nineteenth-century world, labour was so organized that it would not allow wages to go down, and industrialists were so organized that they would not allow prices to go down. Gold was not strong enough to control the new economic forces that were set in motion. The

66

financial crisis of 1931 reflected the fact that new economic forces were too strong to be controlled by a currency system and a financial system of the old pre-War type, and you know what happened. In the attempt to make the old system work, deflation was carried to the point at which it dislocated the internal economy of every country. Its effect was to smash what was at once weakest and most vital in every country in the world. Here it smashed the £ and transformed the political position. In America it smashed the whole of the banking system, with terrible consequences. It has been at the root of the social unrest in France. In Germany it smashed the whole political structure of the State. We had spent our time in trying to restore the gold standard on the old lines. We did it successfully. We were wrong in doing it successfully. We did not realize then that the gold system itself needed to be changed. It has to be changed. It can never, I believe, be the same again. If gold comes back again, it will not be the old tyrant, it will be more like a constitutional monarch representing the economic forces which it has to rule.

I remember a little incident in my own experience of five or six years ago. I was visiting Bombay, a little before the great financial crisis. I saw there an amiable and venerable Indian gentleman, who was president of the Bullion Exchange in Bombay. I went into his office and asked him if he would take me down to see the Exchange. He seemed to be extremely embarrassed and asked if I would come back in a fortnight so that he could make arrangements for me to be properly received. But I said no, I could not. The Exchange was a few doors down the street; why could he not put on his hat and take me down? Still he hesitated. I said, "What is the real reason that you do not want to take me into the Bullion Exchange?" He replied, "I will tell you. You are connected in the minds of the people here with the restoration of the gold standard. A few days ago," he said, "another visitor to the Bullion Exchange was suspected of a similar association, and we are burying him this afternoon." I thought the views of the members of the Bullion Exchange in Bombay were mistaken. I still think their methods of protest were a little energetic, but after five years' further experience of what the unmitigated gold standard system has done, I am at least in a better position to understand and to sympathize with their point of view.

What I have illustrated from the case of gold I might have illustrated from other spheres. The old pre-War system was not, in many vital respects, strong enough or suitable enough for the new forces that had to be controlled in the modern State. In the particular sphere of tariffs our strategy in trying to get rid of State impediments was based upon the assumption of *laissez-faire* in international trade and commerce as normal. Whenever we saw new tariffs, we endeavoured by exhortation and by negotiation to nibble them away and chip them off. We did not inquire what exactly the new tariffs expressed, whether it was not the case—as indeed in some cases it was—that they represented the external counterpart of a new system, whether wise or not, of national control of a national economy. We proceeded to deal with the situation very much as we would have done had we been working not in 1927 but in 1913.

For a long time it looked as if we were succeeding. In 1927 we had the unanimous verdict of that great World Conference that tariffs ought to come down. In 1927 and 1928 they began to come down. Then the resistance began to grow. We did not know quite why it was. There was a new protectionist movement in England; there was an unskilful use of the great bargaining opportunities of the British market. Mr. Hoover's ratification of the higher Smoot-Hawley tariff was a new, unexpected and unecessary impediment to our efforts. We thought our failure was due to such special causes as these. We were wrong. We were defeated by greater but less visible forces. We were like an army making a frontal attack upon a strong but not impregnable fortress, measuring our opponents, seeming to make a little progress here, having some hope of victory, and then, at the moment of apparent success, being blown up by a subterranean mine, of which we had known nothing. What defeated us in 1930, though we did not know it, was the development of those terrific forces which smashed the world system in 1931, but which were already in 1930 driving one country after another back to economic nationalism. So much for past history.

With this experience in mind, how should I now try, in present circumstances, to enlarge the area of international trade? What would be the new policy which I should recommend? Well, I should start by assuming two things. I should assume that the economic forces of the world are now so organized that an externally imposed currency and financial system will not be able again to dominate and control them; that a currency system, a financial system must in future be rooted in the economic forces themselves. I should assume that State intervention in the form of tariffs, quotas and so on, as a counterpart of the domestic economy, will continue. And on these assumptions I should advise policy along the following lines.

In the first place, since the enlargement of world trade requires a reasonably stable medium of international exchange, I would try to get a kind of stabilization. But it would be a conditional stabilization. An arrangement to keep currencies in relation to each other should, in my view, be accompanied by the specific condition that a corrective change in the ratios should be preferred to the enforcement of a policy of drastic deflation. I will not now go into the technicalities involved. Any who are interested can find my proposals in two articles of mine in *The Economist* of July last year. It is interesting to note that a beginning has been made the kind of policy that I then proposed with the arrangement between the American, British and French treasuries when the franc was devalued.

Secondly, I should no longer merely preach that the only thing is to remove impediments to trade and then let the old automatic system effect the necessary adjustments. I should say, "By all means plan your national economy but plan it as a whole; let your policy at least be not less than national. Do not form what you call a national policy out of the mere accumulation of successive measures improvised under the pressure of organized interests. Do not improvise and think nothing of the secondary consequences of what you are doing. Look before you leap." As an example, take the question of the balance of payments, which exactly illustrates the difference in method. Under the old system in 1924–27 we used to say," Do not bother about the balance of payments. Encourage imports and you will get exports; the automatic working of the currency system will secure that." I would not say that now, because I realize the strength of the forces of resistance. I would say, "Consider your balance of payments, but study it as a whole." It is not true,

71

as some people said in the past, that every import necessarily means an export. It is not true that you must always sell as much as you buy and buy as much as you sell. But what is true is that your balance of payments as a whole, if you count not only trade, visible and invisible, but loan operations, *must* balance; what you sell, plus what you borrow, *must* be equal to what you buy, plus what you lend." That is a simple statement to which there is no exception at all. This means that if a country aims at more exports than imports, it *must* be prepared to allow the difference to be lent. It has a choice between certain alternatives. It may aim simultaneously at increased imports and exports, or at reducing its imports and *either* losing exports or increasing foreign investments. But it is arithmetically and materially impossible for a country to have a "positive" balance and stop foreign lending. The attempt to do so, however, may involve disastrous consequences before it is finally seen to be impossible. If countries would aim not at a "positive" balance, but at a balance; if they would give up trying to fight the laws of arithmetic, the consequences would be of inestimable value. For they would soon realize that it would be of definite national advantage to encourage certain classes of imports by reduction of tariffs. A re-examination of each nation's balance of payments on a purely national basis would result in each country finding that it had a considerable number of tariffs which it could afford to remove or reduce. Once it did that, it would have the basis of negotiations with other countries.

Then we come to the method of negotiating, the method of removing tariff impediments. Here, again, in the world as we have it, I would no longer try a universal system. I would try to negotiate group by group with low-tariff countries, and for that purpose I would certainly advocate a modification of the "most-favoured-nation" principle as it is now applied. I think in this country that principle was extremely favourable and suitable in the days when we were a Free Trade country. But if we are to be a Protectionist country with Imperial preference, it is in its present form unsuitable. We have never thought out anew our main principles of policy in the light of our change in the last few years to protection and preference.

Thirdly, I believe in a return to the old principle of equality of opportunity for all countries in the Colonial markets of the world. In the greatest days of the British Empire there were two main bases of safety. One was the British Navy, the other was the principle of equality of opportunity. I think it is an extremely regrettable thing that, just when the navy has lost its power to give the same measure of security it afforded in the last century, we should have destroyed, for very little economic advantage,

73

the other main basis of the safety of our dispersed and vulnerable Empire.

Next, assuming a measure of State control and planning, I think we should attempt by concerted international action to help countries with surplus populations to find external markets. Negatively, for example, the abolition of the quota against Japanese exports to our Colonies would be beneficial. The arrangement between the American and British Governments over the franc is a beginning in positive co-operation. If we proceed from that to co-operation between Central Banks directed to correcting the fluctuations of the trade cycle, if we could then proceed to co-operate for the formation of wider and wider low tariff, or possibly non-tariff groups, we could then gradually, working upward and outward from the present system, construct a new and more stable system under which a volume of international trade, even greater than was known before the War, would be possible. In a word, my new strategy would not consist in a frontal attack upon national economic policies in every form. It would aim rather at making national policies sane and balanced, at liberalizing them gradually and making them compatible with the extension of external trade. In this way we could more easily, I believe, mitigate economic nationalism and economic autarchy. We could, I believe, gradually turn men's minds from attempting to snatch each other's wealth to the much more helpful and remunerative purpose of co-operating in increasing the total wealth to be shared. If this is our goal, we have the great secular movement of economic progress on our side. For now, as never before, it is true that there could be more for all countries, if we utilized the resources of science to increase production, than even the successful could gain by victory in a struggle to seize the wealth of others. And if we look at the cyclical movement, not over centuries, but over recent years, the moment is also favourable. We have now reached a suitable stage on the upward grade of the trade cycle. We are now with the tide in attempting a movement to enlarge world trade; and our own country, now that the currencies linked to sterling cover more than half the world, is in a specially favourable position for giving a lead. The co-operation in regard to the franc might be the first step on that path. I believe that the present method that I have indicated is the right one. This, I think, is the method, this, I am sure, is the moment, and ours I believe is the country that should give the lead.

3

DICTATORSHIPS: WHAT NEXT?

Wickham Steed

THE best way to begin is perhaps to ask how dictatorships came into the modern world, or modern Europe at any rate. Without going back to prehistoric times, I think we shall find that the first dictatorship came in Soviet Russia. Now, I have not read all the works of Lenin, nor all those of Trotsky, although I have read Trotsky's *The Defence of Terrorism*, and I most diligently read, many years ago, the *Communist Manifesto*, written by Marx and Engels in London in January of 1848, in execution of a command or a commission given to them by a Communist Conference held in London in November 1847; and we have Trotsky's word for it that the whole of Marx is in the *Communist Manifesto*.

My own copy of the *Manifesto* came from a well-authorized source; it was given to me by Laura Lafargue, born Laura Marx, the second daughter of Karl Marx, in a translation of which her father had approved. I have it still, and in order not to weary you with reminiscences, I have brought here a summary of it, or at least such parts of it as bear upon our subject to-night.

After pointing out that, thanks to the existence of railways, the proletariat had reached a degree of unity in 1848 among its members which the mediaeval middle class took centuries to attain, Marx and Engels added: "By this means the proletariat is on the way to establish its own rule after it shall have violently overthrown the middle class"; and again: "The object of Communism is not to abolish property in general, but to abolish private property, that is to say, a form of property that can only exist on condition that the immense majority of citizens shall have no property at all." Then at the end it says: "Communism is working for union and understanding between the democratic parties of all countries. Its aims cannot be attained without a violent overthrow of the existing social order. Proletarians have nothing but their chains to lose; they have a whole world to gain. Proletarians of all lands, unite!"

If I remember rightly, there is nothing in the *Communist Manifesto* about "the dictatorship of the proletariat." That phrase crept in later, but certainly it was well established fifty years ago. The idea of dictating, and the reasons for it, may perhaps be found in a statement made by Lenin to the Spanish Socialist leader, I think Fernando de los Rios. It was a statement made by Lenin himself and Lenin said: "Bolsheviks had never spoken of liberty, but of 'the dictatorship of the proletariat.' They exercise this on behalf of the proletariat, which is a minority in Russia, and will continue to do so until the rest of the community submit to the economic conditions of Communism." So, there we have the idea of dictatorship authentically proclaimed by Lenin, with the addendum that Communism has never spoken of liberty.

Now, the first dictatorship in Russia left no doubt of its intentions, of its will, and latterly of its success, in suppressing liberty and private property. This it did mainly, at least as a continuous effort, by taking over from what had been the autocratic Russian State, the old secret police, or Okhrana, which was one of the instruments of Czarist rule. It developed this secret police first as the "Tcheka" and later as the "Ogpu," carrying its technique to a very high pitch of efficiency; and it suppressed quite effectually all its opponents, not always with the gloves on.

Now, against this suppression of liberty and of private property, certain movements grew up outside Russia. The first of these movements that attracted general attention came in Italy. One can understand that in a country like Russia, where the peasant-serfs had only been emancipated for about half a century, where autocratic rule had rarely been tempered, save by assassination, and where no tradition of freedom existed—one can understand that the obvious method of ruling on the part of a militant minority, or the method to be adopted by a militant minority, would be a method of autocratic dictatorship; but in Italy—Italy that had fought a great struggle for freedom and unity throughout the nineteenth century; Italy that had given birth to Mazzini and to Cavour; Italy that had gradually acquired an honoured and a respected place among the nations as one of the foremost exponents of the Western method of governing—this Italy, after a victorious war, suddenly developed this extraordinary form of government called Fascism.

How are we to account for it? One can understand that in the bitterness of defeat, as in Germany, or in the wretchedness of those long years in the trenches through which the Russian peasants went—one can understand that they should take to some form of violent government; but Italy! Psychologically, the reason was this: The Government of Italy had come into the War, or had brought Italy into the War, without any real humanitarian idealism; a very hard and a very foolish bargain had been driven by the Italian Government with the Governments of Great Britain, France and Russia. Under pressure, Great Britain, France and Russia had promised Italy territorial gains which could do no good to Italy and the very promise of which stultified the morality of the cause (that is, the defence of small nations) which the Allies were supposed to be defending. When at length Italy came into the War, really driven there at the last moment by a violent nationalist agitation let loose by D'Annunzio, the people had not got their hearts in the matter, and so they were told: "Ah! See what we shall get! See what we shall get!"

The Italians fought very bravely; they had heavy losses; they suffered an awful disaster in October of 1917; they held their line against the Austrians and the Germans without the actual support of British and French troops, although these were in reserve; and at last they saw victory before them. Then, at the Paris Peace Conference, instead of doing the one thing that could have brought Italy not only an honoured but a very influential place in Europe and in the world, instead of being true to the Italian tradition of working for freedom under liberal institutions, and instead of helping the new states that were then coming to the birth, Yugoslavia, Czechoslovakia, Poland, Roumania, and so on, the Italians turned their backs on this magnificent possibility of leadership, a possibility that would have given them the primacy of influence throughout the Danubian region and the Balkans. They claimed every stone—one cannot speak of every "stone" of their "pound of flesh"—but they claimed every stone that had been promised them on the rocky coasts of Dalmatia and elsewhere; and when they found that President Wilson, and to some extent the British and French Governments, rather boggled at keeping the word that had been given (although the giving of that word had been subsequently overridden by the obligation which the Allies had entered into towards President Wilson and his war aims), the Italian Government exclaimed: "We have been deceived. We have been robbed. We have been defrauded." Thus the Italian Government created, as a means of putting pressure upon its allies, a kind of artificial defeatism which ruined the spirit of the Italian people. Men came back from the trenches and found life hard. There was a good deal of unemployment. Officers found it irksome to go back into civil jobs—when there were jobs. Peasants had been promised land and were sore when it was not given to them. There were a certain number of prisoners of war returning from Central Europe and even from Russia, where they had been slightly Bolshevized. In these circumstances all sorts of movements began in Italy, disorder, strikes, upheavals here, violence there; and amid this situation Benito Mussolini—who was then the editor of a revolutionary syndicalist journal subsidized by the French Foreign Office and by an armament firm at Genoa—had a brilliant idea. He remembered that in the Sicilian Movement, the Sicilian Rebellion or Rising of 1894, little groups had been formed called *fasci*, the name having been taken from the Latin word *fasces*, meaning the bundle of rods into which the Lictor's axe was stuck. He took hold of this idea; and, as the great Garibaldi had always worn an entirely unsymbolic red shirt, Mussolini put his men into black shirts to symbolize the grimness of his purpose. So the black shirts of Fascism began.

The first notable act of Mussolini as Fascist leader was to offer his help to the Italian workmen who seized the factories in Milan and Turin, the beginnings perhaps of a stay-in strike, in 1920, and also to the peasants who had tried to seize the land. The Italian workmen were too hard-headed to accept his offer of help, or of help in defending the factories against the owners, and rejected it. The owners, seeing that the workmen were not violent revolutionaries at all, then turned round and engaged Mussolini and his Blackshirts to break the heads of Socialists, Communists, and all opponents of property. So began Italian Fascism. It was financed by the big banks and big industry, armed by the general staff, and it went forward through various degrees until the famous "March on Rome" in October 1922, a "march" which Signor Mussolini accomplished in a sleeping-car from Milan.

Here was this movement. Could it succeed? There was a great deal of opposition. If you wish really to follow that movement, you cannot do better than read a little book by one of the bravest of living Italians, Emilio Lussu, a former Deputy for Sardinia, an officer four times decorated for valour during the War, a little book published in English called *Enter Mussolini*. It is a masterpiece in its own right; no book throws so much light on the origins and progress of Fascism.

But at last Fascism was established. Then what happened? Mussolini could brook no opposition. He feared the opposition of a magnificent man named Matteotti, a man with a splendid voice and an irreproachable life, the one man who could have led a movement against Mussolini. Matteotti disappeared. Then the King had to choose, amid the revolt of Italian feeling against Mussolini's growing dictatorship and its methods—the King had to choose whether he would entrust himself to this adventurer or send the adventurer about his business. He chose to entrust himself and the fortunes of his Dynasty and the destinies of Italy to the adventurer, with the results that we see.

Now, the murder of Matteotti was the work of a handful of men who went by the then Russian name of "Tcheka," or Secret Police, now known as the "Ovra"; and it is an absolutely characteristic feature of these dictatorships that they cannot govern without a secret police, which rules by methods tantamount to permanent civil war. These methods are inseparable from Fascism or dictatorship, and

83

they are not compatible with anything like human dignity, democratic freedom, or the representation of the people.

The Italian system went on and, little by little, one saw the natural consequence. Movements or systems founded on violence always tremble, and they reassure themselves by arming their supporters so that resistance to them becomes almost impossible. The development of modern arms, the machine gun, even the aeroplane, even tear gas, to say nothing of another kind of gas, weights the scales very heavily on the side of those who possess and are ready to wield those weapons. The old barricades of 1848, of which you have probably read magnificent descriptions in Victor Hugo's great work *Les Misérables*—those things are gone; popular revolt can no longer express itself in those terms; the odds are too heavy against it.

So Mussolini armed his partisans, and spent huge sums in the process. Note the spending; and note this, as another characteristic feature of dictatorships: They may be very efficient at the beginning; there is no wasting of time in a place like the House of Commons, where people talk and talk, and vote and vote, and something sometimes happens, and sometimes does not happen. The Duce, the Leader, the Dictator, gives the word, and the police see that it is carried out. Very efficient! Good Conservatives and lovers of order, without much respect for liberty, are apt to forget that there is a reverse side to it. As soon as public control of finance ceases, corruption creeps in, and it goes on and on. Presently, in order to check discontent at this corruption the forces at the disposal of a dictatorship have to be strengthened. And, as the spendthrift policy develops, there comes a moment when the head of that system and its supporters have to say to themselves: "If we have to choose between an internal smash and a foreign adventure, we will choose the foreign adventure, because in a foreign adventure you can always work up the feelings of patriotism, national sentiment, and so on, and blind or mislead the public to the realities of the position."

We are getting very near to that point in Italy to-day. It was reached—actually reached—last year, and was not least among the reasons which drove Mussolini forward in his Abyssinian adventure. What the end may be we do not know. We know only from experience that a dictator may be able to do everything except cease to be a dictator. He has to go on, and he usually goes on until there is a smash of some sort, as the Spanish Dictator, Primo de Rivera, found; whereas the supreme value of democracy, of the parliamentary system with all its defects, with all its wide margin of inefficiency, is that it does allow a community to change without catastrophe. The margin of inefficiency in a democracy is the insurance premium which that community pays against the risk of utter catastrophe when change is needed.

Now, we come to the third dictatorship, in Germany. The reasons for the rise of a German dictatorship are different from those that may be assigned to the rise of Bolshevism in Russia or of Fascism in Italy. In a very able book written two years ago by the former editor of the *Berliner Tageblatt*, Herr Theodore Wolff, a German Liberal of wide culture and considerable intelligence, there occurs a passage which runs approximately thus: "The fact was that we Germans believed with a touching faith in the invincibility of our armies. We held that they had the secret, a special, an almost mystical, power of compelling victory, as had been done in 1864 and 1866, and in 1870-71; and the revelation at the end of the Great War that the German armies had not been invincible deprived the German people of one of the most cherished tenets of their national faith." This belief, and this humiliation, sank very deep into German hearts; and we can understand it. The Germans had withstood, for more than four years, a world in arms. They had put up a magnificent fight, and yet they were defeated. They had to cede territory; they had to agree to pay reparations. One of my foreign friends once asked a German who had held the position of Chancellor in Germany in the Weimar Republic, why it was that, in the early days of the German Republic, so few steps were taken to make it really a people's republic; why the old officials were left in their places, the officers of the army in their places, and the Junkers on their great estates, and why so very little change was made except the label "Republic" instead of "Empire." The answer of this honest man was: "We were all so obsessed by the idea of revenge that we did not bother about these things." I believe that to be perfectly true, and that, as Mr. Robert Dell has since said, it was the Germany of 1922–23 which deceived so many people who had not known the pre-War Germany; and in 1933, under Hitler, much of the old pre-War Germany came back.

Now how did it happen? Partly by the fault of this country. After the War, at the Paris Peace Conference, Marshal Foch and other French soldiers insisted that if France was to have peace in future she must control or even annex German territory down to the left bank of the Rhine. Against this idea President Wilson, Mr. Lloyd George, the British Delegation and others protested. They said: "Do not create another Alsace-Lorraine the wrong way round. Do not seize German territory to which you have no right, except a certain strategic claim. Do not give the Germans that pretext for rising, banding themselves together, and fighting a war of revenge." Clemenceau, the French Prime Minister. said to Wilson and others: "I agree with you, but I cannot withstand the pressure of these military men unless you will undertake, you, the United States and Great Britain, to come to the aid of France if ever she is the victim of unprovoked attack." Mr. Lloyd George and President Wilson thought this request or this condition reasonable. They signed, with France, the Anglo-American Convention of Guarantee, promising that this country and the United States would come to the help of France against unprovoked attack, until such time as the League of Nations should be able to organize a superior degree of general security.

Then, as you know, for reasons that it would take too long to tell, the United States backed out of the Peace Settlement, did not join the League, and backed out also from the Anglo-American Convention of Guarantee to France; and we, who were not three thousand miles away from Europe, availed ourselves of our legal right to back out also. The result was that the French felt that they had paid for something that they had not received. They became very nervous, and in 1923 they marched into the Ruhr, ostensibly to get reparations, but really to get control of these territories that the soldiers wanted.

Under the impact of this second invasion, the Germans began passive resistance. To finance it, they began to inflate the mark, and in so doing they started a process of uncontrollable inflation which sent the mark, originally worth twenty to the pound, to a point at which you got five thousand million marks for five Renten marks, that is, marks secured on the land of Germany—five instead of five thousand million.

That meant the total ruin of the middle and lower middle classes in Germany, all who had something to lose, all who had a Savings Bank account, all who held Government securities—and most Germans held them, and were obliged to hold them during the War—and black ruin settled upon the country.

At that moment, Adolf Hitler appeared; a curious fellow, not a German, not a German of Germany but an Austrian, a man who I think had never done a real day's work in his life, or had not done until then. Though I was in Vienna during the whole time when he was there, I never met him because he lived in a doss-house all the time. The story of his life in Vienna is a very curious story. An affidavit has been sworn upon it by his companion and helper in the doss-house. The thing he lived for, when he had earned a few shillings, was to go into a coffee-house and harangue people. One day he saw a film, by one Kellerman, called *The Tunnel*, in which a demagogue harangued the people. It impressed him deeply and he said: "I could do that." He has an astounding talent for that sort of thing; and so —after he had gone to Germany, to Munich, where he earned a miserable pittance as a painter, before the War, and, after he had gone through the War—he found the way to the feelings of his people. To them he said: "What? You German people, the noblest in the world, you in whose veins runs Germanic, Nordic, Aryan blood, you are reduced to poverty, to misery! You know not whence your bread will come to-morrow; and why? Because your armies were defeated in the War? No. They were never defeated—Never! They were victorious everywhere, but when they were on the eve of final victory they were stabbed in the back by Jewish Marxist traitors. Down with them! Follow me! Awake! Germany Awake! You shall see! We shall be great and glorious; we will conquer for ourselves the soil we need, and fructify it with our blood; we will teach the world what peace is, not a peace to be gained by the tearful palm-waving of females, but a peace imposed upon the world by the victorious German sword, bending it to the service of a higher Kultur."

Can you see how such a gospel as that touched the inmost fibres of this poor people? How they were promised revenge, riches, expansion, if they would only follow this great leader? More and more they followed him, and you know the story of his ascension. How, after he had become Chancellor, Führer and Chancellor, and had installed himself in power, his supreme ability showed itself. The Social Democrats were somewhat alarmed; they

were a very respectable party—very respectable.
They did not like to be associated with bad people
like Communists, and so Hitler said to them: "Now,
you see, your comrades abroad are criticizing us.
You know, we are not only National Socialists,
but we are Socialists also, Socialists like you. If you
will send your people abroad and tell your comrades not to criticize us, but to wait and see what
we shall do, we will work with you. We only want
to smash these damnable Communists." So the
German Social Democrats, full of faith, took this
advice; and before their emissaries returned from
abroad they were thrashed, smashed, and put into
concentration camps, and some of them killed.

Then it was the turn of the Catholics. Hitler said
to the Catholics: "You see, we want to redeem the
German people from its slavery, its bondage to
these Jewish professors, lawyers, teachers, doctors
and dentists; we want to bring them back into the
Christian fold. Do not oppose us. We shall be able
to work with you, Catholics of the Centre Party.
We want only to clear up these godless Socialists,
and that is what we want you to help us and give
us power to do." The Centre Party ceased to oppose
Hitler, joined in voting him full powers, and then
he proceeded to hit them on the head "good and
plenty." I cannot honestly say that they have not
deserved some of the misfortunes which have since
befallen them.

Then it was the turn of the German Nationalists. To them Hitler said: "But, you see, we call ourselves National Socialists, but we are really Nationalists. The Socialist part of our name and programme was put in to get the people, but we are Nationalists. Now, you Nationalists must work with us and help us to get into power." So Herr Hugenberg and his mighty film concerns, and his industries, and his papers, helped Hitler to get into power. Hugenberg was presently sent to the London Economic Conference as a German delegate in June of 1933, and was allowed and encouraged to put forward a memorandum demanding for Germany expansion to the East, which meant Russia. His memorandum was promptly disavowed in Berlin. So he returned home, was kicked out of office and has not been heard of since. And so it will be with anyone who puts faith in the word of Herr Adolf Hitler.

Do not imagine for one moment that I am accusing Adolf Hitler of insincerity. No. I believe that every photograph taken by a film camera is a sincere picture—only the sincerity is not always in the same direction, or expressed in regard to the same object. His sincerity changes from hour to hour in accordance with the people to whom he may be talking, or whom he may wish to lead into the paths of helpfulness.

So Herr Hitler established himself, and General

Goering and others burned the Reichstag for him and saddled it on to the Communists and Socialists. Four thousand warrants for the arrest of Socialists, Communists and Pacifists, with photographs, had been made out beforehand, and all those warrants were used within thirty-six hours. There is nothing like an intelligent preparation for events before they occur!

Then he won his election that gave him the majority that he wanted. Having got it, he proceeded, he and his police, to organize not only propaganda but the Geheime Staatspolizei, or Gestapo, a secret State police which took lessons in technique from Mussolini, who had taken lessons in technique from the Ogpu of Russia; and to-day the German Secret Police can give points to the Italian and the Russian and beat them both! But we have the same system, the secret police working by delation, by terrorism, by beatings, by assassination, and by extending its operations throughout Europe and, indeed, the world.

Do you think that London is not watched by the German Secret Police? Do you think that there will not be a report of this meeting within forty-eight hours in Berlin?—there will be. The idea of a secret police, setting spies upon everybody, cultivating delation, terrorizing—that is an indispensable adjunct to dictatorships, and their most effective instrument, for they crush the sense of upright vigour in men and women. When one of their acquaintances or friends disappears, one knows not where, people feel that the same thing may happen to them. Read Kipling's poem *The Old Issue*, written about 1900, and read those magnificent lines in which he describes exactly what happens under a dictatorship. The refrain is: "Suffer not the old king under any name." Well, the Germans have got the "old king," large as life and twice as natural.

And now, what next? Thanks to lack of public control, thanks to the suppression of newspaper criticism, thanks to the "co-ordination" of the Press, thanks to the abolition of the right of public meeting, thanks to unlimited power of propaganda, carried out by the cleverest man in Germany—and in saying that I do not mean any offence either to General Goering or to Adolf Hitler, I refer to Dr. Goebbels, quite the cleverest man of the lot—thanks to all these things, the German people do not know, and cannot know, what is going on in the world.

A few years ago Mr. Henry Stimson, Secretary of State at Washington, said: "We rely upon public opinion, the public opinion of the world, to check aggression and military enterprise." Where is public opinion, I wonder, in the sense of a free opinion freely formed with the help of all the information that can be got, in Russia? Where is it in Italy? Where is it in Germany? There is no such thing; and it is the lack of this public opinion, of something to which foreign statesmen or foreign countries can appeal, that makes the situation to-day far more dangerous than it was even in 1914.

Why, the other day General Goering said, with some economy of truthfulness, that if Germany were to-day suffering privations, or if there were not enough eggs or butter, it was because the colonies of Germany had been stolen from her after an unfortunate war, and her gold had been stolen from her for reparations afterwards. Against these assertions, the second of which is demonstrably untrue, because Great Britain and the United States actually lent to Germany more money than she ever paid in reparations, and she "blued" a great deal of it on armaments—against these statements the British Ambassador entered what has been publicly called a friendly protest at Berlin. The form may have been friendly, but the substance was very firm. The German people have not been allowed to know one word of it, or even the fact that the protest was made. On the other hand, when one of the Chairman's colleagues, an unfortunate Communist, of course, of the name of Gallacher, made the other day some remarks not precisely laudatory of Herr von Ribbentrop, Herr von Ribbentrop took his hat and his cane and went to the Foreign Office to protest against such an abuse of democratic privilege, and our imbecile Press published his protest, so that all we other imbeciles might know. That is one difference between a dictatorship and a democracy.

But are "the German people suffering privations"? They are. I will defy the richest country in the world to spend more than £2,400,000,000 in three years on armaments, to pile up a terrific floating debt, and to throttle all trade that is not trade in war material—I defy any country in the world to do that and not to expose its people to privations. The privations are there. German friends have told me that the winter of 1936–37 is comparable, at best, with the winter of 1916–17, and that was terrible enough.

This brings me to some consideration of the question "What next?" Germany has now an army larger, and in respect of aircraft at any rate, more powerful, far more powerful, than her army of 1914. But there are differences. The army of 1914 had been built up during forty-three years of peace, trained by some of the ablest soldiers in Europe, with every man fit to become, after a little war experience, at the very least a corporal or a sergeant. It was only Adolf Hitler, who had other talents, that never brought his promotion beyond the rank of corporal. You cannot conjure up an army equal to that in quality, even in three years, and it is only one year since recruiting was seriously organized. But technically, in artillery, aeroplanes, machine guns and so on, the German army of to-day is very formidable, and there arises the question: All this expenditure, all this money thrown away, or at any rate poured out, what is it for?—What is it for? Is it merely to claim the equality which some Germans say has been denied to them? No. There is a deeper, a far deeper, impulse, an almost unconscious impulse. Remember that the German lower middle class and middle class have been ruined. Remember that the Hitlerite movement grew out of the lower middle class. Its appeal was to them, mainly. Remember that there is nothing that people who have just emerged from the ranks of the so-called proletariat and have acquired a little property of their own fear so much as to be submerged again, and when all that class fears it is about to be submerged, they see a great leader spending money, building up an army, making them march together —is it going to stop there? He tells them that they can take the broad plains of Russia. "What could we not do with the Urals and the Ukraine?" exclaimed Hitler at Nuremberg in September. But even if they could take the Urals and the Ukraine, which cannot be had for the asking, it might not relieve their present distress very much. They may think that there are easier riches nearer at hand.

Let us make no mistake about it. If the Hitler system lasts, it will be compelled to try to reap the fruits of all these preparations, and to reap them, not by some long-drawn crisis of diplomatic negotiations, but swiftly and unexpectedly. Hitler has said, and in this I believe he is perfectly frank, "I should not be like Mussolini who goes and makes his preparations for months and months, and tells everybody that he is going to do it. I should strike suddenly, without warning, with the maximum strength, and then see what happened. That is what I should do"; and that is what he will do, unless he is made to feel that to do it might be even more disastrous than not to do it.

Now, can that feeling be brought to him? Can it be driven into his mind? That is one of the most anxious questions that any country which, like ours, still clings to a belief in the value of human personality, to the right of free speech, to the habit of public criticism, to the cleansing power of breaths of public air sweeping through a constitution—it is one of the most difficult questions that any country like ours can put to itself. People talk of war. Some say: "Never again! Never again! Never will we go into the trenches again. Never will we send our sons to fight at the front." They are talking archaeology. It will not be a question of sending sons to fight at the front; it will be a question of dying in our beds here in London or in other towns, and the question, the problem, in the next war, may not be a problem of organized masses of soldiery at all; it may be a problem of the relative power of public spirit in resistance to sudden disaster.

It may be a problem of civilian *moral*, and the problem may be set, as a thief in the night, before we know where we are.

Now, how can this immense catastrophe which may strike us, and may strike the French (the Russians are not quite so easy to get at), which might strike those brave Czechoslovakians—how can this appalling catastrophe, not only to nations but to the whole of Europe, be averted? How can we help to save the German people? That is our problem, for when Mr. Neville Chamberlain tells us of our new aircraft and of their terrible fighting power, what does he mean? Evidently he means that, supposing enemy bombers got through to London to break up railways and smash up the main roads, to burn gasometers and to poison us all with mustard gas and other delights, our airmen will be going off and doing the same thing to Cologne, Frankfurt, Aix-la-Chapelle and Berlin; and that while Prague is being smashed, Czechoslovakian aircraft will be doing the same thing at Berlin, at Dresden and at Munich; and while Paris is being set on fire by thirty or forty thousand inextinguishable thermite bombs, the French aeroplanes will be doing the same thing to other German cities. What will be the state of Europe after this pretty performance? Some tell us—Lord Beaverbrook for example tells us—"Keep out of it." I think he ought to be condemned to live permanently in London. It is quite nice to keep out of it, if we can—*if we can!* Much better, if we can, to keep *everybody* out of it.

Now, how can that be done? I can see one way only. The War in 1914 came because Germany believed, as her diplomatic documents and the Austro-Hungarian diplomatic documents show, that Great Britain would not intervene in any European war; and as soon as she had that certainty, or believed that she had it, an emissary was sent from Berlin to Vienna, before the assassination of the Archduke, to say to Austria: "England will not come in. Go ahead. Go for Serbia." Well, Germany was wrong. We came in. We were bound to come in. Lord Haldane had known since 1906, as he told me himself, that the first thing that Germany would do would be to go for the Channel ports, and that is why he made the British Expeditionary Force. We were bound to come in when Belgium was attacked. But, had we been able to tell the world, and to let Germany know, there would have been no war in 1914.

Now, why could we not tell Germany? Because the Liberal Party, a great section of the Press and "Society," had been doped with German propaganda to such an extent that neither Mr. Asquith nor Sir Edward Grey dared say what we should have to do, for fear of splitting Parliament and the country. We had to wait until an issue was presented upon which we could be unanimous. To-day we are being deluged with Nazi propaganda in the same sense. What do you think is the real purpose of Herr von Ribbentrop's mission? To make sure that we shall stay out. To make sure that Lord Beaverbrook's wisdom will be the wisdom of us all, and then Germany will say: "Go ahead," after having this time demanded guarantees for our neutrality, for she would not like us to change our minds in the middle of the business. Herr von Ribbentrop has been sent here to get assurances of our neutrality, at least, and of our friendly disinterestedness if Germany strikes East to get the Ukraine and the Urals. I do not think Herr von Ribbentrop will get those assurances. I should not like to go bail for the infallible wisdom of every British minister, but I do believe that most politicians have a wholesome sense, or at least a wholesome fear, of the people and of public opinion. They know what public opinion is, and if we make it quite clear that, cost what it may, we will not stand aside while everything that we hold dear in Europe is being subjected to, or subjugated by, the peculiar form of *Kultur* which Nazi brutality has invented, Hitler will hesitate. France will say: "At last we know where we are"; the United States, which has thrice come towards us, not for intervention but to give support to those countries that were standing against the abomination of war, would not be indifferent. A moral principle would be raised to which all the Dominions would rally; they would rally round us as readily and as whole-heartedly as they rallied in 1914. They will not rally upon any merely negative, closely calculated, British or English policy in Europe. They will rally for a moral principle, as our people will. My answer to the question: "What next?" is: "Inevitable war, unutterable woe, if we are not true to ourselves and do not stand for those principles of human liberty which have made us great." If we do, there may be immense risk, perhaps incipient disaster, but there will be ultimate triumph for Western civilization, ultimate possibilities of progress for our own section of the human race, which, despite Hitler and his Nordic doctrine, is not the worst in the world.

4

THE FUTURE OF SOVIET COMMUNISM

Sidney Webb

THOSE who watch carefully the working of the public mind are aware of a new change in attitude towards the gigantic phenomenon, the Bolshevik State. First there was the almost universal disbelief in the possibility of its continuance. In 1918–20 every Foreign Office and every legation throughout the world, together with every newspaper editor, were certain that Lenin's Government would collapse or be violently overthrown within a few months; or, as the months passed, within a few years. Then it was vehemently denied from 1921 to 1928 that anything really important was being achieved by the incomprehensible continuance of the Soviet Government. It was alleged that the dire poverty of the whole Russian people remained unchanged; that the wretched peasants were being ruthlessly exploited for the benefit of the urban workers and the Red Army, whilst every few years famine stalked through the land. When, in 1934, the abundance of food could no longer be denied, the accusation became one of universal suppression of individual freedom by a tyrannous and ruthless bureaucracy. Stalin was coupled with Hitler in our British and American detestation of dictatorship. Now a fresh change of attitude may be detected. What, it is asked in 1936, is the basis of this astonishing Union of Soviet Socialist Republics, which has apparently achieved, within less than twenty years, such extensive social and economic progress for 175 millions of the worst peasantry and the most down-trodden factory operatives in Europe! Can it be possible that this vast population, unlike all the rest of the civilized world, can go on enjoying an actual non-existence of involuntary mass unemployment; a universal pecuniary provision against all the vicissitudes of life; and a guarantee of effective equality of education and opportunity for every child, irrespective of race or colour or the poverty or affluence of its parents? The amazing gesture of the adoption, in December 1936, of an unprecedented constitution, including all these and many other advantages, is compelling the Western world to ask another question about the Soviet Union. The question is no longer "Will it endure?" but "What is going to be its future?"

Much depends, of course, on whether the U.S.S.R. can remain free from the ravages and brutalization of war. We may be sure that those in command at the Kremlin will do their utmost to keep out of war. We may, I think, be equally confident that, should war come, the highly mechanized, effectively trained, and' amply supplied Red Army will give a good account of itself. Russia shares with the United States the good fortune of being, among all the Great Powers, the most nearly immune from danger of conquest. It is the least exposed to an attack by air upon any vital centre. Even in the longest war the u.s.s.r. would suffer less by stoppage of its imports and interruption of its wealth production than Britain or France, Germany or Italy. The Soviet Union has, during the five years, so effectively organized and armed its Far Eastern province as to convince Japan that China and Inner Mongolia offer a preferable field for slower but possibly more successful penetration. There is reason to believe that, in spite of all the denunciation and abuse of Bolshevism instigated and permitted by the present Government of Germany, the "Higher Command" in that country knows better than to begin by a direct attack on the Soviet Union. Accordingly, I venture on the assumption that, during the next few years at any rate, the progress of the u.s.s.r. will not be seriously marred by war.

To estimate future changes it is necessary first to determine what are the fundamental features of the present. In innumerable non-essentials Moscow, like London, is perpetually incorporating the improvements invented somewhere else, not to mention some not yet adopted in other lands. Such novelties as neon illuminations, trolly-buses, traffic control lights, fountain-pens, one-price stores, wireless weather forecasts, and broadcast opera performances are being adopted or extended every week. On the other hand the more important pattern of social organization seems stable.

But what is this pattern of social organization? It is easy to miss it. More than once a British tourist, returning from a holiday trip to the Soviet Union, has expressed to me his puzzled disappointment at finding Moscow and Leningrad very much like London or Glasgow. He saw the same hurrying multitude of wage-earners and salaried employees in the streets; the same sort of factories and stores busy under the same kind of managerial discipline, without any apparent "workers' control" or equality of income; the same crowds enjoying themselves in the parks or in the picture-galleries, or squeezing into the not essentially dissimilar theatres and cinemas. He was told that the factories and stores, the cinemas and theatres, and the really beautiful Moscow underground railway belonged not to capitalists but to public authorities of various kinds, all of them branches or organs of the "Government." But what difference did that make to the mass of the people? Where was the Communism or Socialism that he had expected?

THE ESSENTIAL BASIS OF SOVIET COMMUNISM

The fundamental novelty in social construction to be found to-day in the u.s.s.r. is the complete exclusion of the individual or joint-stock profitmaker. In every other country the organization and direction of production and distribution of commodities, and even of most of the so-called public utilities, is entrusted by law and custom to the person who, as legal owner of capital wealth, decides what shall be made, by what processes, and when and where. This private owner, or joint-stock company, is moved and guided by the desire to make profit. The sole object of business of every kind in every country except the u.s.s.r. is to produce profit for the owner. A business is deemed successful if it makes much profit. It is a failure if it makes no profit. In the Soviet Union profitmaking is a criminal offence, punishable by imprisonment for a long term. What would elsewhere be called business is carried on in the u.s.s.r. by individuals receiving salaries or wages, without the motive or stimulus of profit, and also without its questionable guidance.

WHAT IS PROFITMAKING?

The criminal offence of profitmaking in the u.s.s.r. includes two operations which in every other country are rewarded not only by wealth but also by public

esteem. This couple of crimes are respectively stig-
matized by the Russians as "speculation"—meaning
any buying of commodities with the intention of
selling them again at a higher price; or as "exploitation"—meaning any hiring of any person (whatever
the wage) for the purpose of selling the product of
that person's labour for the employer's pecuniary
advantage. The essential change brought about both
by Socialism and by Communism, as the Russians
understand these terms, is thus, what Sir William
Beveridge has aptly termed the "Marxian operation"
on the body politic, the complete extirpation from
the social organism of the motive and stimulus of
private profit, whether obtained by buying and
selling, or by making gain out of the labour of one's
hirelings.

NOT NECESSARILY GOVERNMENTAL

It is this abandonment and penalizing of profitmaking, whether by speculation or by exploitation,
and not any particular form of government or system
of property ownership, that fundamentally differ-
entiates Moscow and Leningrad from Glasgow and
London. Thus the Socialism or Communism at
which the Soviet Union aims is not intelligently
expressed by the phrase by which the idea
was commonly propagated in Great Britain, the
"Nationalization of the Means of Production, Dis-

tribution and Exchange"; not even when, under the influence of the Fabian Society, nationalization was made to include municipalization. The Soviet Union has not vested all the capital wealth of the U.S.S.R. either in the Central Government at the Moscow Kremlin, or in the Governments of the seven (now to be eleven) States of the Union, or in the seventy or eighty thousand provincial, district, municipal or village soviets or councils. These governmental organizations, together with the trade unions, the Consumers' Co-operative Societies, the innumerable educational institutions, the vast medical and hospital services, together with the theatres and parks and other organizations for amusement and sport all of which have their own separate administrations, themselves employ at salaries and wages nearly thirty millions of employees, who are essentially servants of public authorities. But there are also in the U.S.S.R. several millions of independent individual producers—handicraftsmen; inventors; freelance journalists and authors, who simply sell their copy to any public authority; unsalaried artists of every kind paid by fees; prospectors of minerals; hunters and fishermen on their own account, and even a remnant of isolated peasant agriculturists. More interesting are the (possibly) ten or twenty millions of members of *artels*, or co-operative productive societies, themselves making in partnership every kind of household requisite or article of clothing; the members thus working in textiles, leather, wood, iron and lacquer, and occasionally even working their own small mines of lead or coal. Even more numerous are the members of the quarter of a million collective farms or fisheries (*kolkhosi*), in which nearly twenty-five millions of households unite in co-operative partnerships for their main crop or product, whilst conducting as independent individual producers their subsidiary enterprises in pig and poultry, dairy and garden products, beehives and winter handicrafts.

We are still sometimes told that under Socialism the State must be the only employer! As a matter of fact, more than one half of all the adult inhabitants of the Soviet Union find themselves outside the ranks of public employees, even in the widest sense of that term. They are not in receipt of wage or salary at all, but work on their own account as handicraftsmen, fishermen or agriculturists, calling no man master, but producing, either each for himself and family, or jointly as partners in co-operative productive societies (*artels* or *kolkhosi*); after payment of the Government dues, selling their own products freely to consumers at the best price they can get. What is objected to in the U.S.S.R. is not the production, by individuals or co-operative partnerships, of as much as ever they can make for their own use or enjoyment; and not even their production for sale to consumers at the highest prices that consumers are willing to pay—provided always that in the production or distribution no labour is employed for hire. Least of all is there any objection to any person getting for his own labour by hand or by brain as high a fee or royalty, wage or salary as any one of the tens of thousands of separate managements of governmental authorities may consent to give him.

Lenin and his colleagues had in 1917 no particular love for collective ownership for its own sake. It was in order to get rid of the making of profit out of the hiring of labour, with all the power over the wage-earners and all the control over the kinds and methods of production that the capitalist employer necessarily possesses, that the land and railways, the banks and factories were taken out of private owner-ship and vested in the community. What was more remarkable was that Lenin believed and foresaw that this substitution of a planned economy for the competitive scramble for profit would lead to an actual increase in the aggregate productivity of labour. In 1917 no economist in the Western world imagined that the elimination of competitive profit-making could possibly result in greater initiative and inventiveness in all fields, increased investment and rationalization by the captains of industry, when they were merely employed at salaries; augmented zeal and diligence among the rank and file of manual workers, when the trade unions arranged the wage rates, and positively a larger dividend per head among a larger number of workers by hand and by brain than had ever previously been distributed throughout this one-sixth of the surface of the globe. In 1936, less than twenty years later, this is what the economists who deign to look at the u.s.s.r. are now enforcedly recognizing.

And the progress in material production has been during the past decade at least equalled by the advance in the physical health and cultural development of the people, whose numbers have gone on increasing each year—in spite of the so-called famines of which we still hear from enemies of the regime—by about as many as the whole of the rest of Europe put together. The crude death-rate has been reduced below two-thirds of what it was under the Tsar, whilst the infantile mortality has been halved. The children in all the settled areas have been got to school, and literally millions of adolescents into the higher colleges. In some respects the educational institutions are ahead of those of other countries. The visitor in 1934 to an elementary school in a rural village found the children of twelve to fourteen being quite effectively taught German; and then discovered that, already in every school in the cities, in every village school in the Ukraine, and in a rapidly increasing number of villages throughout the rest of the u.s.s.r. (in fact, in all the "seven-year" schools, which will within a couple of years be universal from the Baltic to the Pacific), either English or German was being taught. He had to confess with shame that in not one village elementary school in England was any foreign language being taught. At the end of 1936, two years after this observation in the Russian village, there is still no village in all England that can show the same achievement.

Of the rapidly extending organization of theatres, concerts, cinemas and educational lectures throughout the Soviet villages I have no room to speak; nor yet of the enormous number of books and periodicals printed and sold in the hundred different languages of the u.s.s.r., where there are also literally tens of thousands of free lending libraries. The various social services, which are now mostly administered by the trade unions themselves without any individual insurance payment by the workmen, are more extensive and more costly than those of Great Britain or any other country. And, most important and most significant of all, there has been since 1930 no involuntary mass unemployment among able-bodied men and women in the whole length and breadth of this immense country. Nor is such unemployment expected to recur. This fundamental economic problem has, it is claimed, been finally liquidated! The trade unions and the local authorities undertake to find a job within his or her capacity, at trade union rates of wages, for every applicant; or, in the alternative, for young people, to admit them to training for skilled work with maintenance until qualified.

This is not to say that even to-day the aggregate wealth production in the U.S.S.R. is as great as that in the United Kingdom or the United States; or even that the amount per head is as great. But the aggregate product is less unequally shared. Even so it would be difficult to prove that the average Russian mechanic or factory operative, agricultural worker or fisherman is as well off as his British or American colleague *when in regular employment*. But the Russian wage-earner is clearly better off, both materially and culturally, than he has ever been before, and his condition is still rapidly improving. There is indeed good reason to expect that, within another decade, the inhabitants of the U.S.S.R. will be on the average distinctly better off than the average wage-earner in the United Kingdom or the United States.

THREE MAIN FEATURES IN THE SOVIET PATTERN

Now, pursuing our examination of the characteristics of the U.S.S.R., there are three marked features in the Soviet pattern of social organization of which it behoves us to take notice.

THE FUTURE OF SOVIET COMMUNISM

MULTIFORMITY

There is first its definite multiformity of structure and function. Least of all countries is the U.S.S.R. a land of uniformity. Its industries, its crops, its minerals, its fisheries actually rival in diversity, if they do not even exceed in number, those of the most highly developed nations of the world. The social form taken by all these varied exterprises exhibits an extensive variety from the isolated individual handicraftsman, through a diversified array of co-operative partnerships and municipal departments, up to the single centralized bureaucracy to which the direction is entrusted of the most widely extended railway network that exists in the whole world. Even in political administration the eighty thousand soviets proliferate into the most outrageously different structures, ranging from the rudimentary administration of the sparsely populated village within the Arctic Circle up to the complicated maze of municipal organization on which the life of Moscow's four millions depends. Throughout the U.S.S.R. there is an outstanding diversity in race, in language, in habits of life, and even in religion. To all sections of the population "cultural autonomy" is guaranteed. And with a steady and almost universal advance in civilization, coupled with an ever-increasing unity of patriotic devotion to the Soviet Union as a whole, there is, so far as I have been able to judge, no sign of any abandonment, or even diminution, of this fundamental characteristic of multiformity. During the past decade it has certainly increased.

UNIVERSALISM

No less marked in the Soviet pattern is its persistent drive for universalism. Whatever improvement or advance is made in any department is promptly extended to every part of the U.S.S.R. in which that department is operating. All the backward areas, even all the backward races, share immediately in every extension or development of public education. In fact the expenditure from federal funds on education, like that on the promotion of health, is actually greater per head of population among the backward races than it is among the Russians or the Ukrainians. This is very different from the practice of all the capitalist empires, whether British or Dutch, French or Portuguese; and even of all the capitalist States that are not empires but are divided into social classes, whether Germany, the United States, or Switzerland. The same striving for universalism is manifested in the geographical location of new mining and manufacturing enterprises. These are distributed over the wide area of the U.S.S.R., not solely according to the prospect of a maximum economy of production in particular localities, nor yet to their degrees of immunity from foreign aggression; not even preferentially according to the extent of the lessening of the burden of transport upon the overworked railway system; but also very largely in such a way that no considerable area shall be left unprovided with alternative opportunities for the local employment of its inhabitants. I see no sign of the abandonment of this principle of universalism in the future.

PARTICIPATION

The third of these well-marked features in the Soviet pattern of social organization is the constant insistence, throughout all collective activities and every branch of social life, on the widest possible participation. Not only is the political electorate the widest in the world, but it is now being cleared of all remaining exclusions and inequalities. In the trade union and co-operative organizations, with their tens of millions of members, the meetings are more numerous and frequent than in other countries, but also they are habitually attended by a majority of the membership and by women equally with men. The daily administration of the public services in populous cities as in rural villages is largely undertaken, not by the salaried officials, not even mainly by the elected councillors themselves, but, without remuneration, to a considerable extent by private citizens as part of their voluntary social service. Fifty thousand men and women are reported to be habitually thus engaged in the city of Moscow. The moral obligation of every citizen to devote spare time to voluntary public service of one or other kind, of his or her own choice, is constantly being impressed on the adolescents of all occupations, and is very generally fulfilled. It is, of course, not so much for the sake of increased efficiency in the public administration that this duty of participation is insisted on; indeed, it is not to be believed that it secures greater efficiency than would be obtained by an adequate civil service, trained and loyal, if such could be provided. What is claimed is that this universal active participation in social service is an indispensable element in any genuine democracy. Where everything is done for the people without effort by themselves, and nothing by the people, not for their individual selves but for the common good, all the electoral machinery in the world will not create a democratic community.

THE NEW CONSTITUTION

The most impressive onward stride towards the future of the Soviet Union is the enactment, after the most elaborate popular discussion that the world has ever witnessed, and eventually practically without dissent, of a new and extremely democratic constitution for this huge State. Nearly all the Press comments have failed to emphasize the most important of the innovations of this constitution. Thus the method of direct election of representatives by the largest electorate ever known already prevails in city and village alike, no fewer than seventy-seven million votes having been actually cast for the Soviets at the last election out of a total electorate of just over ninety-one millions. Universally direct election was actually included in the published programme of the Bolshevik Party as long ago as 1903. It is true that amid the revolutionary turmoil of 1917–18, and the incessant labours at reconstruction during the past dozen years, it was almost necessarily arranged that the members of the four or five thousand district and provincial councils, like those of the supreme assembly, the All-Union Congress of Soviets, should be indirectly elected, just as members of the Senate of the United States used to be. It is not clear to the outsider how much difference has been made in the character and composition of the United States Senate by the substitution of direct for indirect election. No one can predict with any confidence that any greater difference will be made by the analogous change in the u.s.s.r. Even the adoption of secret voting in substantially equal constituencies of considerable magnitude in place of the show of hands in relatively small meetings, may not improbably be found, in the circumstances of the u.s.s.r., to make very little change.

Similarly, with regard to the enlargement of the electorate and the equalization of representation of citizen and villager. Certainly the gesture is impressive of the abandonment of all exclusions and inequalities from the electoral franchise. Neither ill-gotten wealth nor former anti-social occupation, not even family relationship to the late Tsar, nor membership of a religious order, will henceforth deprive a Soviet citizen of his vote. It has scarcely been noticed that most of these exclusions had already lapsed in practice. It is true that without any change of official policy towards theology, nearly fifty thousand practising priests of the Greek Orthodox Church, together with some hundreds of Roman Catholic, Evangelical, Mohammedan, and Buddhist ministers, now for the first time receive votes. But what are fifty thousand in an electorate that has already reached a total of more than ninety millions? Moreover, the vote of each of the sixty odd millions of rural electors will henceforth count for as much as that of each of the thirty odd millions of urban electors, instead of only about half (usually misstated as one-fifth) as much. This is Stalin's effective answer to the constantly repeated slanders as to the oppression of the peasants. These are confidently expected to vote in much the same way as their sons and daughters and brothers and sisters now resident in the cities.

But to the student of political science the most important innovation is, not any reshaping of the electoral machine, but the enshrinement in the constitution of a new set of "rights of man." The Declaration of Independence of the American rebels of 1776, and the United States constitution of 1787, were both founded on an almost unfettered individual ownership of private property for the purpose of profitmaking. The French Declaration of the Rights of Man in 1789 (and as rewritten in 1793) had a similar basis. These were alike sanctifications of the motive of profitmaking, then believed to be the necessary foundation of economic progress. Even in the *Principles of a Civil Code* Bentham allowed only one encroachment upon private property—that of taxation—and recognized only four "ends" of civil government without specifying how they could be attained, namely individual subsistence, security, equality and abundance. In 1848 Louis Blanc asked in vain for the addition of the "right to work," meaning the right to be found employment by the State. In 1936 the Soviet constitution ensures to every citizen, not only protection against aggression and arbitrary arrest, but also the right to have remunerative work; a specially elaborate provision for motherhood; the right to specified hours of rest and paid weeks of holiday; the right to education of every kind and grade and at any age, free of all charges; and, most far-reaching of all, the right to full economic provision, according to need, in all the vicissitudes of life. What is even more important is the fact that the inclusion in the constitution of these enormously extended "rights of man" is but the explicit consecration in the constitution of what is already in operation over a large proportion of the area of the U.S.S.R.

It may be convenient to give in tabular summary —not in the phraseology of the Bolshevik translations from the Russian, nor even in the exact terms of the original, but in those which will enable the British reader to understand what is meant—the twelve "Rights of Man" consecrated in this new constitution:

(i) The Right to Elect, irrespective of race, sex or colour, freely, directly, secretly, equally and universally, at 18 years of age, to all governing assemblies from the lowest to the highest, without pecuniary or other limiting qualification.

(ii) The Right to Criticize every branch of the public administration, and to agitate for its alteration, by public meetings and by printed matter, for which accommodation, paper and printing will be provided—yet without freedom to individuals or factions to resist or obstruct the execution of what has been at length finally decided on by the supreme elected legislature.

(iii) The Right to be free from arbitrary arrest.

As in other continental administrations, there will not be, what is so much cherished in England, the special protection of that British peculiarity, the Habeas Corpus Act. But (Article 127) "the citizens of the U.S.S.R. are guaranteed inviolability of person. No person may be placed under arrest except by decision of a court or with the sanction of a State Attorney" (meaning the judicial department of the Procurator, which is now to be independent of the executive).

(iv) The Right to Freedom of Speech, Freedom of the Press, Freedom of Assembly and of holding mass meetings, and Freedom of street processions and demonstrations. These "rights of the citizens" by Article 125 goes on to say, "are ensured *by placing at the disposal of the toilers and their organizations* printing presses, supplies of paper, public buildings, the streets, means of communication, and other material requisites for the exercise of these rights.

(v) The Right to Work, and to be enabled to live by the work that must be found for all able-bodied adults, with option to join in co-operative production societies, either in industry, agriculture or fishing.

(vi) The Right to Leisure, by due limitation of the hours of labour in office, factory or mine; together with the provision of paid holidays and of all approved means of happily using the leisure so ensured.

(vii) The Right of those who work at wages or salary, and of their incapacitated dependants, collectively, to the entire net product of the labour so employed throughout the whole U.S.S.R. as annually ascertained by Trade Union and Sovnarkom (Cabinet) agreement.

(viii) The Right to Positive Health of body and mind, so far as this can be secured by the widest possible use without any fee of preventive and curative medicine and surgery, and of public sanitation, with wages in sickness and incapacity without "waiting time" or limit; and the ensuring of adequate nutrition and physical training to all infants, children and adolescents.

(ix) The Right of Women to fulfil the function of motherhood with all possible alleviation of the physical suffering involved; without pecuniary sacrifice or burden, and aided by universally organized provision for the care of infants and children.

(x) The Right to prompt and adequate provision for the family on the death of any breadwinner; with gratuitous funeral, and instant succour of the home.

(xi) The Right to Superannuation before senility or upon breakdown.

(xii) The Right to Education equally for all races, without limit or fee, for persons of any age and either sex, with maintenance in suitable cases.

Considered as a political gesture, alike to the millions at home and to other nations, the diplomatic world privately allows it to be magnificent. Even the most sceptical of gentlemanly attachés will not avoid being shaken in his conviction that Bolshevism cannot possibly endure. The student of political science tabulates a brand-new specimen in the way of constitutions. But, of course, constitutions are judged, in the long run, not by what they say but according to how they work—or are worked! The "Twelve Tables of the Law" enshrined in the new constitution of the Soviet Union, as it is enacted in December 1936, will be judged by the world according to the way in which these provisions are found to be actually working, say in December 1941, after five years' experience without war! What we can say at present is that they at least point in what seems to most Britons and Americans the right direction.

THE VOCATION OF LEADERSHIP

The first four of the above-mentioned "Tables of the Law" cover, it may be said, all that nineteenth-century Liberalism regarded as fit matter for any written constitution. Curiously enough, it is upon the future construction of and the faithful adherence to these four that the sceptic in other lands entertains most doubt. He notes that there is nothing in the new constitution to end or even to weaken the effective leadership of the people which has made the Communist Party practically supreme in the Soviet Union. How can the new constitution, the British or American Liberal asks, be regarded as a charter of liberty when it is plain that a single "party" maintains an effective monopoly of the initiation of policy, if not actually of high public office? Can the existence of such a potent apparatus of leadership, however democratically constituted, be reconciled with anything that Great Britain or the United States understand by political democracy?

It must here be noted that, by the quite usual mistranslation of Russian terms into English, or the different use of the Russians of terms previously borrowed from the Western democracies, what is called the Communist Party of the U.S.S.R. bears the very smallest resemblance to what is known as a political party in the United Kingdom or the United States, France or Scandinavia. It does not seek to enrol in its membership all those who seek to join, or who profess adhesion to its cardinal tenets, or agree to vote for its actual programme, or are prepared to subscribe to its funds. It does not attempt or aspire to enrol in its membership all the citizens, even a majority of them. On the contrary, the Communist Party of the U.S.S.R. rigidly limits its membership to a tiny fraction of the electorate, at present under 3 per cent. Admission to membership is granted only after a period of probation, which may last for years, during which the character, assiduity, zeal and intelligence of the candidate are watched and tested. He is held to a higher standard of personal behaviour than can be expected from the average citizen. He pledges himself to an acceptance of a voluntary "poverty," to the extent of not retaining for himself and family (apart from the functional expenses incident to his office) more than a prescribed maximum of salary; and to implicit obedience to any definite command of the corporate body to which he has, at his own request, been admitted. For any breach of these two fundamental rules, and for any scandalous misbehaviour or backsliding, he will be warned and reprimanded, and eventually expelled. But the corporate body is and remains essentially a voluntary organization, entirely outside the law; and though now—for the first time—mentioned in the written constitution, it is given no powers by that instrument, or by any other statute. It is, in fact, more like a religious order than anything that the Western world understands by a political party. It may be accurately described as an organized vocation, analogous to the vocation of medicine or the vocation of the so-called clerisy, which takes upon itself the function of intellectual leadership of the community in all matters of public importance. That leadership is exercised by persuasion; through the example and precept to their fellow citizens of the moiety of the membership which continues to work at the bench, the farm, or in the mine; and through the direction of policy in the execution of the powers legally vested in the other moiety of the membership, comprising such members as have been elected or appointed to public offices.

How effective and wise may be the leadership by which the Soviet Union is definitely guided in policy, and how widespread may be the virtual ratification afforded to that leadership by the popular participation in the actual administration that is so marked a feature of the pattern of social organization of the u.s.s.r., may well be a matter of dispute. What has to be said here is that, so far as I can discern, there is at present no sign of any passing away—none even of any diminution or important alteration—of the practical dominance over policy throughout the Soviet Union of its unique Vocation of Leadership, exercised by the peculiar voluntary organization which the Russians call the Communist Party.

PERSONAL FREEDOM

More important, however, than this or that definition of democracy is the question of personal freedom. Leaving aside any quibbling about terms or their verbal definitions, the substantial issue is whether the indication, for the future of the Soviet Union, is towards greater or lesser freedom for its individual citizens than at present exists. But what are the conditions of freedom?

What is not always remembered is that the freedom of the individual, and the individual's own consciousness of freedom, alike depend jointly on the absence of restraint and on the presence of opportunity. To the rentier living on interest or rent, or the professional living on fees or royalties calling no man master—even to the wealthy entrepreneur or financier—what matters is the absence of restraint. To the wage-earner in any community of highly organized industry or agriculture, commerce or finance, the mere absence of restraint seems but a mockery of personal liberty unless he enjoys, along with freedom of thought and utterance, also the opportunity to gain a continuous and reasonably secure livelihood for self and family. The freedom of any highly evolved community, if it is to be more than an empty word, can be nothing other than the aggregate of the individual freedoms of all its members. It is hard to believe that this aggregate will not be the greater the nearer the material and social conditions of all its members approach to equality. The Bolshevists claim that, taking into account both restraints and opportunities, the aggregate of individual freedoms of all the 175 millions of the U.S.S.R. is to-day positively greater per head than the corresponding aggregate per head of the British Empire; and even than that per head of Great Britain or the United States. This claim cannot at present be statistically tested. But it may fairly be said that there is much reason for expecting that, if there is going to be any continuance of the present rapid growth of its material prosperity, the Soviet Union will in another decade or so be able to demonstrate beyond cavil its superiority, in a greater aggregate per head of individual freedoms, over any highly evolved large State organized on the basis of capitalism and the direction of wealth production by competitive profitmaking, with all the inequality of wealth and social conditions involved.

But what will be the future in the U.S.S.R. as regards the treatment of heretics, rebels and obstructionists of the policy of the Government for the time being? There is first the question of the treatment of persons guilty of high treason or political assassination. Western critics find it hard to approve the angry condemnation to death of successive blocks of "traitors," even after public trial, and the incomprehensible "confessions" of the accused. A philosophic comment is that any hard-fought and successful revolution leaves all parties in the new community still bound in a certain pattern of behaviour formed in the revolutionary struggle. Not until the revolutionary generation passes away will that pattern entirely fade out. For years some of those who resent any particular government policy will from time to time be tempted to try to effect a new revolution. For years some of those who happen for the time being to control the government will harbour the gravest suspicions about their opponents' loyalty. What may, we think, be hoped is that, with every increase in the certainty of governmental stability, and with every proved success of the administration in raising the standard of life, the ferocity of the repression of traitors will abate—to be succeeded more and more by popular ridicule of individual reactionaries and the kindly seclusion (as of homicidal lunatics) of any apparently incurable disturbers of the established order.

More important in the long run to social development than the dying away alike of sputters of new revolution, and of the ferocity with which these are put down, may well be the effect upon the minds of original thinkers, especially in the social sciences, of the public habit of insisting on orthodoxy. In Japan, to cite an extreme case, public opinion seems to support the Japanese Government in preventing any scientific inquiry which may cast doubt upon the direct descent from the sun of the human being who for the time being holds the office of Emperor. Such a repression of scientific inquiry cannot but interfere with the candid study of genetics and anthropology in Japan, and therefore with the discovery of new truth. Something of the same popular intolerance of criticism and free investigation is felt to exist in the Soviet Union, not with regard to the ancestry of any of its leaders, but with regard to the scientific validity of some of the theories or doctrines on which the Soviet social order is based. How stringent and how effective may be this intolerance at the present time is hard to estimate. What is important is the prospect for the future. My own view is that in the U.S.S.R. of to-day tolerance in intellectual matters is apparently greater than it has been in the past, and that it shows signs of further widening.

If I may sum up this lengthy, though very inadequate analysis in a sentence, I would say that at the close of the year 1936, when nearly all the world seems staggering towards social and economic catastrophe, the U.S.S.R. stands out from every other country as supremely the Land of Hope.

5

THE NEXT WAR: CAN IT BE AVOIDED?

P. M. S. Blackett

WHEN this lecture was planned last June, we had just seen the end of one aggressive war, the Italian aggression in Abyssinia. A fortnight after I wrote the synopsis, the next aggression had started, this time in Spain. We are now watching a war in progress in Europe, and, though it is not yet the general European war of the title of this lecture, it may become so quite soon.

It is not possible for me to give a detached and academic survey of the present state of affairs, and I do not intend to try. For one thing I am no expert on this subject. I am neither an historian nor an expert on foreign or military affairs, nor an economist. But I will try to be as realistic as I can in my account of the present situation, not with the idea of striving for an impartial objectivity, which I cannot attain, but from the point of view of immediate political action.

I must inevitably begin with the events in Spain, not only because of their immediate importance, but because they show some new features in European history, which we may perhaps see repeated elsewhere. The Spanish struggle may be taken, in some respects, as a dress rehearsal of future events in Europe—or perhaps it may already be the first act of the drama.

Now the facts about Spain are hardly in dispute. The legally elected Government of the People's Front has had to take up arms to repel a military revolt, backed by a reactionary aristocracy and a politically powerful Church. Owing to the unexpected uprising of the Spanish people, this revolt was defeated in the main towns, and would have probably been suppressed in a month or two all over Spain, but for the help that was given to the rebels by Fascist Italy and Nazi Germany, in collaboration with which countries the plot was planned. In spite of that help the rebellion would probably have been defeated by now, if the British and French Governments had not denied the Madrid Government the right to buy arms, to which it was legally fully entitled.

What has happened in Spain, as was said recently, is rather like the French Revolution in reverse. The Spanish Government is fighting to defend what the French Revolution achieved in France, and what this country achieved a century or two earlier. The freedom which England won in the time of Henry VIII from the political power of the Vatican, and the curbing of the power of the monarchy and of the aristocracy by Cromwell, were the essential basis of England's rise to power and prosperity. Even the Conservative newspapers admit in their less guarded moments that the Madrid Government is fighting against the power of a landed aristocracy and a reactionary Church, which have kept the Spanish people one of the poorest, the least educated and the most illiterate of the peoples of Europe.[1] I do not think there can be any denial of these facts.

It is interesting to note the attitude of the British Government to the struggle. Not a single word of sympathy towards the Spanish Government has been uttered, as far as I know, by any member of the British Government. On the contrary, our Government has, by its action in collaboration with the French Government, effectively given support to the rebels, and this has led Franco to within an ace of victory. It has done this in flat opposition to every imperial, national and democratic interest. It has staged the farce of the Non-Intervention Pact in London, an episode which will go down to history as one of the most contemptible for which we have been responsible. A

[1] "According to the latest census made in 1930, 45·5 per cent of the population could neither read nor write."—*Spain in Revolt*, Gannes and Repard, p. 228. "In 27 out of 50 provinces registered in 1931, 76·5 per cent of the people owned 4·7 per cent of the land, while 2 per cent owned 67 per cent of the land." *Ibid.*, p. 217.

fitting comment on the work of this Committee is given by the Berlin correspondent of *The Times*, who wrote on November 18th:

> "Meanwhile those responsible for German foreign policy are wondering whether they cannot get the Non-Intervention Committee to put an effective control on arms going to Spain, now that assistance is going to the other side."

The full consequences of this betrayal of every democratic and imperial interest are still to be felt —and will certainly involve more arms, less security, and very likely an extension of the war to the whole of Europe.

It is necessary to analyse in more detail what is behind the support of Franco by German Nazi-ism and Italian Fascism. This support is not given for love of the Spanish Nazis, but for the simple reason that Nazi-ism and Fascism intend to attack democracy throughout Europe, and—very sensibly from their point of view—they intend to attack it at its weakest link, and the weakest link is Spain. If Franco wins, France will have a third Fascist frontier to defend. She already has two. She will be weakened on the Rhine in consequence, and since, as Mr. Baldwin has said, our own defence is on the Rhine, our own defence system will also be weakened. If Franco wins, the British Navy will have to abandon the Mediterranean. And yet many

Imperialists here applaud Franco's progress. The support of the rebels by Hitler and Mussolini is thus no accident but a deliberate attempt to cut France off from her African colonies and so weaken her that she will be absolutely unable to do anything in the West of Europe to prevent Hitler doing what he wants in the East.

But this is not the only action being taken towards the same end. German agents are now intriguing in French Morocco with "patriotic" French reactionaries to help them create a Fascist movement there. This would still more weaken the French military position, by making impossible France's reliance on her colonial man power. It is widely believed in Paris that if Franco wins, a Fascist rising in France is not at all improbable—many say it is almost certain. And, no doubt, true to type, it will be financed and encouraged by Hitler and Mussolini.

It is difficult to gauge the exact degree of responsibility of the English and French Governments for the policy of denying to the Madrid Government the aid to which it was legally entitled. In Paris, it is stated quite definitely that England threatened to abandon the mutual guarantees under the Locarno Pact if complications arose through France aiding Madrid. Mr. Eden denies this. The best that can be said is that everything has happened exactly as if England had in fact made her threat.

Now, those who do not approve of the policy of

the National Government, and who did not vote for it at the last election are, in a sense, not responsible for its policy. But I must admit to a sense of acute shame at the part played by the Left in this country during this crisis. It would surely have been possible for the Labour Party, with its great organization and power, to have obtained the reversal of the decision to ban arms if it had really wanted to do so. If it had organized a mass movement of its supporters in July and August, it could have got that policy reversed. Actually the French Government has used the attitude of British Labour to justify the non-intervention policy to its own supporters.

If this is a true picture of the position in relation to Spain, what are we then to expect for the future? The Nazis and Fascists have the initiative in Europe. So the problem is "What will Hitler do?" Here, naturally, we leave facts and come to hypotheses, but I do not think there is very much doubt about the type of events which the future has in store. Essentially in Nazi-ism and Fascism there is a drive to war—for reasons both economic and political, some of which are clear, and some of which are not so clear. There is a continual drive for markets and raw materials in a highly industrialized country; then there is the creed of aggressive nationalism required to cover up the fact that the Socialist part of the National Socialist programme has not been carried out. Only by such a creed can the people be got to accept the sacrifices which are necessary for the vast armament programme that is being carried out. These are some of the theoretical reasons for political aggression. In practice the facts are clear. Japan, perhaps not technically Fascist but nearly so, Italy and Germany have all made war-like aggressions within the last few years. Japan's aggression in Manchuria was applauded by our patriotic Right; Italian aggression in Abyssinia equally so. Within three months of the end of the Italian campaign in Abyssinia the next Italian aggression starts in Spain. And there are some who think that by giving some colonies to a Fascist country you can stop them wanting more!

Of course there is a drive to war latent in all highly-industrialized capitalist countries and not only in the Fascist ones, but there is an enormous difference between those which by the luck of historical good fortune have great reserves and therefore do not feel the need for aggression, and those other less fortunate countries. For these and other reasons, at the present moment, Fascism and Nazi-ism are in an aggressive mood, while British capitalism is not.

As far as I can see, every prophecy of the last two years has proved too optimistic. Between the blind optimism of most of the Government and of the Opposition and the openly pessimistic warnings

of Mr. Winston Churchill and the Communists—
they both agreed roughly on what Germany would
do—the latter have been proved right. I see no
good reason to believe that I may not prove to
have been sketching the future again too opti-
mistically.

Now I want to consider, in a little more detail,
Hitler's probable policy. There is evidence enough
in *Mein Kampf* of Hitler's intentions. Admittedly
this book was written many years ago under the
stress of imprisonment, but the passages in it where,
for instance, he speaks of the necessity to annihilate
France, have not been expunged.[1] This book is
circulating by the million in Germany. Then there
are numerous other books teaching a religion of
aggressive nationalism. And at the Nuremberg
Conference there was the violent anti-Soviet
campaign.

An interesting private letter[2] from a Spanish
diplomat who sided with the rebels has recently
been published.

"We know that Italy and Germany will never
allow the Spanish Government to win, even if
90 per cent of the population is behind it. The

[1] Many important extracts from *Mein Kampf* are collected
in *Germany's Foreign Policy*. Friends of Europe Publication,
No. 38.
[2] *The Week*, October 7, 1936.

nonsense about Fascism not being an article of
export has long since been abandoned, and to-day
it is Italy and Germany who protect the Fascist
regime in smaller States. What does it matter
what the population want, or how they fight to
maintain it? The armaments of Germany and
Italy are invincible and they are fully at the
disposal of Fascists in other countries. It is not
the rebels whom the Spanish Government is
fighting, but the German and Italian Empires.
France and England are far too frightened of
these two powers to intervene for the Government
and we feel sure of its overthrow."

Another private letter, from a German official,
may be quoted:[1]

"Everything points to a revolutionary foreign
policy. None of our contradictions can be solved
internally; everything forces us to an international
conflict. If it lasts more than a year, I believe
the regime will go to the dogs. This is also the
opinion of the Nazis, and it is essential to remember that German strategy of the coming war aims
at a speedy annihilation of the enemy. Only a
long war will turn into a civil war."

The Berlin Special Correspondent of the *Morning
Post* wrote recently:

[1] *The Week*, October 28, 1936.

"That Hitler will be forced to make war rather than face an internal collapse and revolution, is nevertheless the opinion not only of most outside observers, but also of many sober-minded Germans themselves."

It is also Mr. Winston Churchill's view.

Hitler's policy at the moment consists, to a great extent, in the semi-peaceful penetration of smaller States, rather than in the waging of open war. By propaganda, bribery, encouragement of local Fascist movements and so on, he is getting his tentacles into other countries. The events in Spain are, of course, a conspicuous example of this policy. The Rexist Movement in Belgium is reported to be financed from Germany, and the leader, M. Degrelle, is said to be an ardent admirer of Hitler. This is a new technique by which Nazi diplomacy tries to break its enemies from within.

In the forefront of Hitler's open policy is a violent anti-Soviet campaign. This is a very interesting and important fact. For I think that if one were to consider the best possible policy for Hitler to pursue, in order to reach his ultimate end, which is the pan-Germanic domination of Europe, one would in fact propose the policy which he is pursuing. By means of a violent anti-Communist campaign, Hitler is trying to get accepted as the saviour of Europe against Bolshevism. If he succeeds in convincing his neighbours in the West to accept him in this role, then the rest follows, for they will, one by one, fall under his domination. Then he may, or may not, carry out the aggressive military campaign against Russia. The anti-Soviet propaganda campaign is an admirable move for Hitler to play at the moment. But I think there is a certain amount of evidence that he may not actually make the final move of a military campaign.

It is certainly the hope of many British Conservatives that Hitler may expend his admitted aggressive energies on the U.S.S.R., leaving the west of Europe in peace. But it will be remembered that in the quotation given from the letter of a German official, reference is made to the necessity of a short war. The Nazi System is extremely strong on the surface, but it is not certain that it has the staying power which is necessary for a long war, and which the democratic countries possessed in 1914. Now a war against Russia must be a long war. The geographical difficulties of a war against the U.S.S.R. are immense. For one thing, there is no common frontier; air power would certainly not be decisive, for the distances are too great, the population too sparse, and Russia's heavy industry is too far away. Thus a war against the U.S.S.R. cannot be a short war, and Germany must have a short war. I doubt, myself, therefore whether it is safe for a British Conservative to take it as assured that Germany can be induced to expend her aggressive energies in the East. But much of British policy seems based on this assumption.

I want now to consider the position of Germany as against the British Empire.

On the one hand we have a country arming to the limits of her industrial power, with unemployment reduced to a small figure, with factories working shifts day and night, and restrained by nothing, except the difficulty of importing enough raw materials, from arming indefinitely. And there is the implicit belief on the part of the Nazis—which include the great majority of the middle classes— that Hitler can give them everything. He asked for arms and he got them. He took the Rhine without asking. He has asked for colonies, and they believe he will get them. The campaign for colonies is coming increasingly into prominence as a motive of Nazi policy, stimulated, of course, by the Italian success in Abyssinia. And it is clear that it is mainly at the expense of British Imperialism that Germany's demand for colonies could be satisfied.

The Nazis have a certain contempt for this country. I think they have some reason for it. England is a rich country, with the highest average standard of life in Europe, but with a large part of its population underfed. Is it not reasonable that Hitler should have some contempt for a rival imperialism which, though very rich, does not take the trouble to feed properly the people on whom its own safety depends?

Thus though Hitler will undoubtedly continue the anti-Bolshevik campaign it is not certain that he will really expend his energies only in the East. In fact, it has been easy to predict that he would be likely to turn West; it is now not necessary to predict this, for he has done so. Since Hitler turned West by his support of Franco, the last hope of the success of a reactionary isolationist policy for Britain, that is that security can be bought in the West at the price of a free hand for Hitler in the East, has been disappointed. For the attack on Spain is an attack on the whole position of British Imperialism, and not only in the Mediterranean.

When we came to observe the reaction of British Imperialism to this threat to their interests, we came across one of the most extraordinary phenomena of modern times. This curious story has been told very brilliantly in a recent article by Sir Norman Angell[1] under the title of "The New John Bull." It is natural to expect a Conservative Government to behave like a Conservative Government. One does not—or did not until these last few years —expect a Conservative Government to throw away everything for which it had previously fought. One did not expect to find the reactionary Press applauding the aggressors against their own interests; con-

[1] *Political Quarterly*, vol. 7, p. 311, 1936.

gratulating Japan when she challenged British interests in China and encouraging Mussolini to embark on the invasion of Abyssinia. The Italian success in Africa is certainly the greatest blow to British power and prestige that has been struck in many decades, and the argument, from an imperialist point of view, against supporting Franco in Spain seem to me unanswerable.

This fact of "imperialism in retreat" is a very important new development and has profound social consequences in connection with what I am coming to later—the position of the political Left, and the Labour and Peace movements in this country.

Now why did British Imperialism encourage Japan, Mussolini, Hitler and Franco? The reasons are rather complex. There is no doubt at all, for instance, that one of the driving forces behind the proposals of the Hoare–Laval treaty was the desire to prevent the fall of Mussolini; the fear of what may happen if dictators fall is certainly one reason why British Imperialism fears to press its own interests too strongly against aggression. In the case of Japan there was the hope that Japan would hinder or destroy some part or all of the power of the u.s.s.r. Then fear on account of our supposed military defencelessness has played a large part in the inaction of Britain in the last year. Again, capitalism fears war, because it knows it may not survive another. Then any success of the Popular

Front in Spain is feared on account of the encouragement it would give to a similar movement here. Then some part of the governing class is openly Fascist; another part would apparently throw away the Empire, if, in order to save it, it is necessary to support Democracy and the League of Nations.

Now the whole future of this country, and of half Europe, depends upon how far this retreat will go. It may be argued—and many Pacifists would like it to be true—that this retreat means that British Imperialism is in fact about to resign, that it has given up the attempt to hold the position that it built up in the nineteenth century, and that it is prepared to let this country sink to the level of a second-class power, and hand over its colonies and trade routes one by one to any dictator who asks for them. If that were the case it would fit in quite well with the view of many extreme Pacifists, who think anything better than fighting, and who would rather be nazified quietly, than take active steps to stop the Nazification of Europe.

But I do not believe this is a real possibility, even if there are some who think it desirable. I believe the retreat of British Imperialism is limited in extent and time, and that it fully intends to fight in the end to defend its world position. Though I think that its leaders are completely and hopelessly misguided in their tactics, and that they are, in fact, behaving unintelligently in relation to their own

WHAT IS AHEAD OF US?

interests, I believe that they will fight in the last trench, when they see unquestionably their Imperialist position being threatened.

For instance, *The Times*[1] says:

"But any act of aggression against any part of the British Empire or its communications, or in the neighbouring parts of Western Europe, will be met by Great Britain with the full force of her armed resources, and elsewhere by participation in such common action as occasion may demand."

British Imperialism is rearming because it intends to fight, and fight to win. For instance, Sir Samuel Hoare tells us that Britain will defend her position in the Mediterranean. To combine this policy with that of effective support of Franco is simply stupid.

We must consider now what were the avowed objects of the policy of the National Government in regard to Spain? The non-intervention policy was introduced partly because, it was said, it was what Madrid wanted. This appears to have been untrue. Then it was introduced partly because, it was hoped, it would shorten the war. It has not done so. Again it was said that the policy was the best way to avoid international complications. Far from doing so, the international complications are just beginning. Whereas in July or August a quick victory for the Madrid Government would have

[1] *The Times*, October 26, 1936.

148

ended international complications at once, now it is very difficult to see how the Spanish situation can be settled without a major international explosion.

I have put forward the view that the foreign policy of the British ruling class in relation to the aggressive action of certain States has been stupid in relation to its own interests and also disastrous to the interests of democracy. Now I must raise the question whether perhaps I have not been too critical of them. Perhaps they are really intelligent and far-sighted.

I think that if the history of the last twenty-five years is considered there is little evidence to be found that they are either intelligent or far-sighted. It is the same people who muddled us into the war of 1914, in their own Imperialist interests. Before 1914, one German cruiser on the African coast was almost enough to start a European war.

The war we fought for four years was a war between rival Imperialisms—a war for markets, power and prestige. And now the same ruling class seems to be throwing away everything that was won. The same people who refused the chance of peace in 1917, who imposed the incredibly disastrous Treaty of Versailles on Germany against the protest of the Left, who snubbed and cold-shouldered the really democratic Germany which arose out of the War, and which so many of us learned to love, now give away, one by one, half the things that they made a million of our countrymen die for, twenty years ago. And the position is infinitely more serious than it was then. Imagine what would have happened if England had been defeated by Germany in 1914. England might have been occupied, an indemnity would have been paid, but eventually the nation would have revived. What would happen now would be the Nazification of Europe and of England. This would mean the end of Democracy in Western Europe, the subjection of Europe to a crazy racial doctrine, and to a vast militarization which would probably end with a general assault on the u.s.s.r.

The final conclusion of this analysis is this. Hitler will dominate Europe unless stopped by force. The present policy of the National Government will not prevent it. On the other hand, it will not lead to peace for this country, but rather to a final war in defence of its Imperialist interests, but under impossible tactical conditions, with no allies, and the result will be defeat. There is perhaps some excuse for the comment of a French colleague on the British Government's policy:

"Those whom the gods wish to destroy they first make mad."

If one admits these facts and probabilities—and, as I have said, every recent prognosis has been over-optimistic—what is to stop the Nazification of

Europe? Germany is a highly industrialized, highly disciplined State, peopled by 60 million extremely intelligent people, trained to believe in war as an ultimate good. Great Britain is a democratic un-military nation of 45 million people with an Empire to defend; France has but 40 million people, is not so highly industrialized, and has already two, and perhaps soon will have three Fascist frontiers to defend, and she has her local Fascists in her midst. So what can stop Hitler? Obviously by a strong League policy, France and England would bring in behind them a great number of the smaller States. But they are not enough. There is only one military counterpart to Germany in Europe to-day, and that is the u.s.s.r. Without the aid of the u.s.s.r. there will be Hitler over Europe and over the British Empire as well.

It is interesting to note that the u.s.s.r. has taken on the role that Britain had for many years—that of defender of small nations against big, of democracy against tyranny. England, the first country to have its middle-class revolution, and consequently the first country to begin its industrial revolution, had adopted this role consistently for many years. She has now abandoned the role completely, and the u.s.s.r., the first country to have its proletarian revolution, has taken up the mantle England has thrown down. It is somewhat ironical to have to comment that if the Madrid Government wins and if, therefore, British Imperialism retains its hold on Gibraltar and the Western Mediterranean, it will be almost entirely due to the help given to the Spanish Government by the U.S.S.R., and by the magnificent band of European anti-Fascists who, with the active disapproval of their Governments, have made their way to Spain to fight Fascism. The stopping of Franco when already in Madrid is one of the most dramatic incidents in European history, and may prove to have had a decisive importance, comparable only in recent times with the Battle of the Marne and the repulse of the White Russian Armies from Leningrad and Moscow.

Eighteen months ago or so, France, on the initiative of the French military staff, made a pact with Soviet Russia—a mutual assistance pact within the League of Nations. The French military staff are not Bolsheviks, but they realize clearly that the growing aggressive power of Germany has to be met by force, and that the U.S.S.R. alone can help them. One of the immediate reasons for the conclusion of this pact was the Anglo-German Naval Pact, signed a few months after the decision at Stresa to consult with France and Italy over all measures that concerned mutual interests!

The tragedy of Abyssinia was another consequence of the Anglo-German Naval Pact. France was so alarmed by England's behaviour that she thought she could not trust England to back her against

Germany. Laval felt it unsafe therefore to antagonize Mussolini and so made certain that sanctions against Italy should fail.

It is very important to consider the question of the military strength of Soviet Russia. She is the greatest industrial country of Europe to-day, and has a population two and a half times as great as Germany; much of her heavy industry is many miles outside the range of bombing attack; she has very strong fighting services, especially in the air, and a disciplined population which believes, and rightly, that the future is with them. This is the power that the French military authorities have brought in for purely military reasons to redress the balance of Western Europe. It is well to remember that England is now trying to get France to abandon this Pact of Mutual Assistance with the U.S.S.R.

The policy of the country seems to be to let Hitler have a free hand in the East. What is really wanted is a Mutual Assistance Pact between England, France and the U.S.S.R. to prevent Hitler having a free hand in the West! He has already started aggression in the West. If France went Fascist—I do not think this will happen, but if it did—I think even our Government would see the wisdom of a Soviet Pact, as the sole chance of saving the Empire.

When we now turn from the policy of the National Government to that of the Labour Party, we find an almost complete paralysis. The political Left in this country has had very little effect on the international situation during the last year. In spite of the Peace Ballot, in spite of the uprising of opinion over the Hoare–Laval affair, little of permanent value has been achieved. The only exception to this is the appreciable success of the campaign for medical assistance to the Spanish Government, and the small but important contingent to the International Brigade sent from this country.

I want to try and to analyse why the Left is impotent in this country. There appear to be a number of reasons.

Firstly, I think there has been much too much concentration on stopping this country from waging an aggressive and imperialist war. A small but effective mass movement in the London Docks on a small scale did, it is true, check England from supporting a war against Russia in 1920. But the tactical situation is much more difficult now. In this epoch of "Imperialism in retreat," the Right take up an isolationist attitude tending almost to pacifism, while the Left, who want to stop aggression by force, take on the role—in the view of the Right—of the warmongers. The task of the Left, if it is to have any effect at all, is clearly to force the Government of the country to stop aggression by threat of force, and this means to take the risk of war.

THE NEXT WAR: CAN IT BE AVOIDED?

The policy of the Labour Party over Abyssinia and again over Spain has certainly involved a risk of war. Two consequences have followed. The pacifist mentality of much of the Left has hedged, being unwilling to face the facts of the new situation. And the Right have been able to say, "You want to lead us into risk of war on behalf of every oppressed nation and yet you will not face the military consequences." The problem of the Left in this country now is no longer to stop the Right from waging an aggressive imperialist war in its own interests— it has no intention of doing this at present—but it is to get the Government to stand by the system of collective security; this means stopping aggression by threat of force. It is true that such a policy as the Left are advocating means a risk of war; but the policy of the National Government means a certainty of war, in which Britain is also certain to be defeated.

Democracy cannot be defended by those who will take no risks. It is perfectly clear that if Fascists believe in their creed and will fight for it, and if Democrats believe in their creed but will not fight for it, Fascism will win.

I think it can hardly be denied that if the Labour Party is to take on its true function of leadership against Fascism in Europe, it will have to make great changes in its organization and policy. At present it is not only practically stagnant, but is losing the enthusiasm and even the support of its members. Its attitude to the Spanish situation seems typical of its timidity and complete lack of real leadership.

What is wanted, in my view, is a strong Government of the Left, willing and able to resist Fascism, in alliance with the other League powers; and these are primarily France and the U.S.S.R. Very many of the smaller powers would follow such a lead with a sigh of relief. The events of the last few years show that the National Government can certainly not be relied on to do this, because of its hatred of Russia, and because it is frightened of acting in collaboration with Left Governments abroad.

The potential and international problems that would face a Left Government are huge, and would have to be faced with determination and courage. Mr. Maisky, the Russian Ambassador, said, "You have got to organize peace; you have got to pay for peace; and in the last resort you have got to fight for peace," and M. George Dimitrov said, "All recent events, and first and foremost the lesson of the Spanish events, go to show that the time has come when all means, including the use of arms, have to be employed to defend Democracy against attack by the Fascists." Since I believe this to be true, I believe also that more arms, particularly in the air, are necessary for this policy to be carried out. I certainly do not trust the Government to carry it out, but it is not safe to wait to create the arms until a Left Government gets into power. For arms take a long time to produce and the danger is immediate. There would be a very great danger of the paralysis of a Left Government, through its belief in its military defencelessness. The fighting services would have merely to hint that they are not able to defend the country to paralyse completely all international initiative by the Left.

There certainly is a chance that the increased armaments will be used in aid of Fascist powers and against Democratic ones and against the U.S.S.R., but I believe this risk is less than that of a Left Government finding itself impotent through lack of arms. I also believe that it is easier at the moment to influence effectively the direction of foreign policy than to alter the fact of rearmament.

How can we get this strong and determined policy from the Left? What is wanted is obviously the active help and work of every sincere anti-Fascist. But it is essential not to let the names "People's Front," or "United Front," become merely slogans with no precise meaning. It seems to me that the essential basis of effective action by the Left, first and foremost, is a united working class, and that means definitely, as the first step, Communist affiliation to the Labour Party. Many Liberals will, it is to be hoped, bring in their wisdom, experience and organizing ability, but they are not and cannot be, now in the twentieth century, a sufficiently homogeneous class to bear the brunt of such a policy, which has many risks attending it and which must be drastically carried out if it is to succeed. It is necessary to start with a united working class; that is an essential first step. The faith, hope and discipline of the Communists is an essential part of the French Popular Front, and must also be an essential part of a similar movement here. Just as the military power of the U.S.S.R. is an essential part of any effective international anti-Nazi policy, so also is the aid of the Communist Party an essential basis of an effective internal progressive policy.

It is not possible to wait for the next General Election to begin serious political activity. Hitler will not wait. This emphasizes what appears to me to be one of the fundamental weaknesses of the Labour Party's conception of opposition. It thinks too much in terms of general elections every five years and it seems to think that government is carried on merely in Parliament. That is a very naïve view—real government is not only carried on in Parliament, but in business houses, in offices, in banks and in the stately clubs, where, as a wit once said, "One cannot hear oneself speak because of the noise of the grinding of axes." If the Opposition is to be effective, it must act in the country and in the street as well as in Parliament. This is how the

French Popular Front was built up. Unity must be created in the street. It must be created in all kinds of organizations and movements, large and small, and when it has been created, it will be able to gate-crash into the timid parlours of the Labour Party.

It is very interesting to find the importance of mass political movements stressed in a place where one would least expect, in a Sunday paper. I found the other day an interesting remark.[1] "The danger of war lies not in our commitments—Sir Samuel Hoare, indeed, denies we have any—but rather in an explosion of popular anger over some too cynical act of aggression." Clearly the writer has in mind the Hoare–Laval affair, and it is realized that there is a limit to what even a powerful Government can put across. This writer realizes the fact that, on important issues, government is in the streets. But spontaneous, unorganized acts of popular fury, like those of which the Hoare–Laval Treaty was the occasion, are not enough. That explosion succeeded in its immediate object, and had absolutely no effect a month later.

Now the question is, how best to organize the mass opinion of the Left in order to have the desired effect. If it is not possible to get a progressive Government into power immediately, all possible effort must be put into a campaign to alter the present foreign

[1] *The Sunday Times*, "Scrutator," November 15, 1936.

policy. To do this it is necessary to organize mass feeling on all the immediate issues before the country, and in this way to bring together all the latent political forces the Left.

Both social issues and international issues must be used. The agitation about the distressed areas has been a very good example of how courageous leadership by the Communist Party has succeeded in organizing a movement which had a great political effect. Another point of extreme importance about which to organize political feeling is the scandal of malnutrition which has been brought out so clearly by the recent researches of Orr and McGonigle. It is interesting to note that the talk during the War about England being a C3 nation has been largely forgotten, till it is found that enough men cannot be got into the Army owing to the poor physique of the population. So again, with the approach of a war situation, the health of the people is talked of again and Conservative papers have leaders about the tragedy of the distressed areas. The Government scheme of physical training is one of the reactions to this revival of awareness of the nation's bad physique. Physical training is valuable, but good nutrition is the first essential. However, it is cheaper to give men physical training than to feed them.

The rearmament programme of the Government gives an excellent opportunity to make effective political demands, both internally and especially in relation to foreign policy. Effective working-class leadership could certainly use the excellent tactical situation created by the Government's demand for co-operation in rearmament to force the country's foreign policy in a direction favourable to the Democratic powers and to the U.S.S.R.

On these and such other social issues it is necessary to build up a mass organization of the people—in spite of the disapproval of the official leaders of the Left— they will come in afterwards, as they did in France.

Then the international situation must be used, which means the Spanish situation first and foremost at the moment, because here is an issue which really does appeal to a large part of the English population. It must be pointed out again and again that the present policy of the Government is suicidal from their own point of view, and that their defence policy is open to very serious criticism. For instance, a Mutual Assistance Pact with the U.S.S.R. would immediately reduce the danger of a possible air attack on this country to, say, one-fifth or one-tenth straight away, because Germany, the only country likely to attack us, would have to keep a large part of her forces in the East. Collective security is clearly the only possible way to keep the arms budget within reasonable limits. There is again a very great reason to fear a partial repetition of the mistake of the 1914 policy of not

L   161

making clear enough what the policy of this country is. It must not be supposed that the Government is united on these issues. They are not all acquiescent in German aggression. Mr. Winston Churchill is quite clear-headed about the German danger. He writes, "Unless there were a front against political aggression there would be no settlement. The next twelve months would be the last chance of averting a European conflict and of preventing that conflict from darkening into a world war." Then again he expressed the view that if Britain replaced collective security by an arrangement with Germany, it would mean one of the most fearful wars of history.

The object of this policy is not the encirclement of the German people, for whom one cannot but have a profound admiration and sympathy. The original Mutual Assistance Pact between France and Russia remains open on entirely equal terms to the German Government. But the encirclement of aggressive Nazi-ism is the essential basis of peace in Europe.

It follows from this view which I am putting forward, that if we are going to stop Hitler dominating Europe, we have, first of all, to force this Government—if we cannot replace it—to carry out a strong League policy and to strengthen the League by a Mutual Assistance Pact with the U.S.S.R., with the object of stopping military aggression in Europe. If this can be done, Europe will have a breathing space. But this is not enough: the root of the trouble remains, the drive and urge of the Fascist powers towards expansion; merely to put a steel ring round German aggression will not solve the European problem. At the moment there is no such ring; the Nazis are going from success to success, and with every success their claims become greater.

Is there any hope of doing more than this, of ending the Fascist drive to aggression before it leads Europe into a world war? I think there is. It is true that one cannot but feel rather pessimistic sometimes. One sees the rigid, unified, powerful Fascist States canalizing every possible economic activity to war, and one finds the Democratic States rather half-heartedly, and disunitedly, following the same road. But under the surface there is more hope to be found.

Exclusively national loyalties, even when fostered by years of violent propaganda, are not complete. There is rising in Europe a new international loyalty, not of Geneva or of statesmen, but of the common people, especially of those who have suffered under Fascism. The part that the International Brigade played in saving Madrid at the last minute is an example of how the people of Europe themselves can, if they take action on their own account, effectively check Fascism in Europe. The Democratic Governments of Europe refused to help the Spanish Government, the Fascist Powers helped the rebels. But people of Europe, both from Democratic and Fascist powers, went to the help of Spanish Democracy on their own account, taking great risks to do so, and they changed the whole situation.

All this was done without the full support of the organized working classes of Democratic Europe. Much more can be done if we can get a united working-class movement in this country, joining up with the united working-class movements in the rest of the world—it is the British which stand out against this at the moment and block the way to unity—if we can get this, there will be a basis of appeal to the German working class itself. They are not nazified—not all of them, by any means. The Fascist strength is rather superficial. We have to get through that surface. A united working-class movement, based on united trade unions, can get this appeal across the Nazi frontiers by propaganda, by direct appeal, by sanctions. Already the news of the successes of the International Brigade before Madrid is circulating in Germany, and is having an appreciable political effect. In this kind of way there is a chance that Hitler can be stopped before he has made his final aggression, which will plunge Europe into war. This is, I think, the only hope. In a real sense, the future of European civilization depends on the German working class. But their potential force for peace can only be brought into effective action when the rest of the world's Democratic forces are united to help them.

6

PLANNING FOR HUMAN SURVIVAL

Lancelot Hogben

MR. COLE began this course by asking, Can capitalism survive? I propose to end it by asking, Can the human race survive? In stating the subject of the lecture in these terms, let me insist that I shall not attempt to make any prediction about future events. I am a scientific worker. It is not my province to prophesy. Science is content to prescribe recipes for conduct, as where to put a telescope to see Pluto or when to turn up at the observatory if you wish to see it. Prediction is the prerogative of bookmakers, evangelists of a four-square gospel, and professors of political economy.

The survival of human beings depends on two things, the rate at which they die and the rate at which they are born. Science has increased our knowledge about agencies which affect both. It thus offers us increasing scope both for death control and for birth control. We can kill people more swiftly and on a far more generous scale than our ancestors could do, and we can keep many more of our babies alive. We know much more about how to regulate the rate at which babies are born without fear of exhausting the plenty potentially available for all. We can also decide to stop having them altogether without undue personal inconvenience. Knowledge of either kind may be used for good or evil. For instance, the United States is making war on citron bugs with poison gas and aeroplanes. Hence no sane person would suggest that the Labour Party's distaste for war as an instrument of international policy betokens a hatred of science. One might also expect no sane person to regard well-informed concern for the consequences of declining fertility as a repudiation of contraceptive amenities. Unfortunately very few birth controllers are sane in that sense. Death controllers of Hitler's kidney are singularly intolerant towards people who are still glad to be alive, and most birth controllers are fanatically enraged when they meet people who want to keep the human experiment going. Nothing here said will prevent them from misunderstanding what I shall say later on. If I preface this lecture by stating that I am in active sympathy with contraceptive practice, I only do so for the pleasure of demonstrating how few people can recall what they have heard half an hour before.

Professor Blackett has given you his views on death control in the preceding lecture. I shall confine myself to birth control. Most people have enough imagination to realize that there now exists a vast potential of destruction without parallel in human history, that the fate of civilization will probably depend on the attitude we adopt towards it, and that it has made the issue of sheer survival a pivotal concern of statesmanship. Few people are sufficiently familiar with the less heroic facts about fertility to realize that civilized mankind is now faced with a new potential of sterility, that the fate of civilization will depend on the steps we take to deal with it, and that it is likely to dominate all other issues of social policy in the near future.

I do not propose to go into great detail in stating the facts concerning population growth at the present time. They have been amply set forth in two books by Dr. Kuczynski, *The Measurement of Population Growth* and *Population Movements*, in Enid Charles's *Twilight of Parenthood*,[1] in Professor Carr Saunders's *World Population*, and in the *Struggle for Population* by David Glass. If their significance has attracted little comment in the realm of political discussion, it is doubtful whether there is any branch of social studies in which there is more complete unanimity about the facts themselves. The facts may be summed up in one brief statement. The level of fertility in the more highly industrialized countries has now sunk below the limit at which no concomitant fall in

[1] Now reissued by Watts and Co as the *Menace of Underpopulation*.

mortality can prevent a continuous decline of population, unless people can be induced to have larger families. There are several reasons why this prospect fails to excite alarm. One is that the form in which public statistics of population are presented is apt to mislead people about what is really happening. One is that we have scarcely thrown off the Malthusian mythology. We have had too little time to adjust ourselves to an age of potential plenty. A third is that many prevalent views about declining fertility are based on rationalizations of personal sentiment belied by the statistical data available.

Two features of the public statistics contribute to the complacency which most people display. The first is that population has not yet begun to decline steadily in any country. The second is that the birth-rate conceals the most relevant features of the problem. The birth-rate gives the number of children born per annum per 1,000 members of the population. By itself a fall or rise in this tells us nothing about the reproductive capacity of a population. This is easily seen if you consider two populations both composed exclusively of females who have had or will have the same number of children in the course of their lives. If in the same year one community is exclusively composed of women of childbearing age and the other is half made up of individuals younger than fifteen years or older than fifty years of age, the number of births in the second

will be roughly half as great as the number of births
in the other. Consequently the birth-rate of the first
for that year will be twice as great as that of the
second.

The right way to decide whether a community
is capable of replacing itself is to measure fertility
by the number of girl children born on the average
to one woman in the course of her reproductive
life. This can be done when public statistics record
the age of the mother at the birth of each child.
In England and Wales at the present level of
fertility one hundred women on the average have
eighty-five daughters in the course of the entire
child-bearing period. There would thus be a 15 per
cent deficit of replacement in each generation even
if every daughter herself survived to become a
mother. In other words no further fall in mortality
can arrest a continuous decline, and nothing short
of immortality can safeguard us against extinction,
unless fertility is raised by somewhat more than
15 per cent. This would not be achieved even if all
women married, unless the average married woman
had more children.

You may ask: why then do the Registrar
General's returns still show a slight annual increase
in the population of Britain? Leaving migration out
of account the reason for this is that there is a
necessary time lag before a fall in fertility exerts its
full effect, if mortality is falling at the same time.

That such a time lag may occur is easy to see with the help of a fictitious illustration. Imagine a community in which every woman dies at the age of sixty and produces one female offspring in the course of her life. The female section of this community would be numerically stable as long as this fictitious state of affairs lasted. If a certain proportion of women became sterile while mortality remained the same, the annual births in the succeeding year would be less than the number of deaths. It might happen that mortality would not remain the same. For instance, we can imagine that all women of nearly sixty might live to be nearly sixty-one. The number of annual deaths would suddenly drop in the ensuing year. So there might be an excess of births over deaths in spite of the contemporary drop of fertility. If mortality persisted at the new level, the proportion of older people in the population would increase to a certain limit and the population would continue to grow for some years; but if the average number of girls reared by the women remained less than one apiece, the population would eventually begin to decline and continue to do so. The character of population growth in modern industrial communities resembles this fictitious situation in so far as it depends on a simultaneous fall of fertility and mortality. The fall in the latter can only check the effect of the former *temporarily*. An extension of the average duration of life beyond the child-bearing period has no effect on the *capacity* for further growth.

At a fixed level of fertility and mortality about sixty years elapse before the full effect of a lower fertility begins to operate. If no females died before fifty, and if the present level of fertility were kept constant, at the end of sixty years our population would be falling off by 15 per cent in a generation. Comprehensive estimates of the consequences of declining fertility on the future course of population in Great Britain have recently been made in the Department of Social Biology by Dr. Enid Charles. If fertility and mortality remain indefinitely at their present level the population of England and Wales will be reduced to one-half its present size a hundred years hence. By then it would be declining at the rate of 25 per cent per generation, and would be reduced to one-fifth its present size two hundred years hence. If fertility and mortality continue to fall off at the rate suggested by the experience of the last two decades the population of England and Wales will be reduced to one-tenth of its present size a century from now.

Before lightly dismissing the prospect which is disclosed by these figures, other facts deserve attention. Some are contained in an as yet unpublished study carried out by my colleagues. During the last twenty years, the percentage fall in fertility has been greatest in those sections of the population with the highest fertility at the beginning of that period. In other words the differential fertility of the prosperous and poorer classes is rapidly disappearing. In its inception the fall of national fertility was mainly due to a change in that of the relatively well-to-do. Since the latter form a relatively small section of the population, fertility is almost certain to decline more steeply in the next two decades. So any estimates of the prospect of a rapid decline in population such as those given by Dr. Charles are likely to prove conservative.

Sooner or later any Government, Socialist or otherwise, will have to face the task of raising fertility or to accept a downhill retreat to racial extinction. A few more figures will help to show the magnitude of the undertaking. At present marriage, death, and sterility rates, the maintenance of a population at a fixed level demands a mean completed family of nearly three children.[1] Although a Labour Government could easily halve the infant death toll, if (among other things) it were resolute enough to replace the higher officials at the Ministry of Health, it is quite certain that no juggling with death or marriage rates would reduce this estimate appreciably below two and a half.[1] To maintain an

[1] Dr. Kuczynski gives the following estimate. In Denmark the net reproduction rate computed on the basis of fertility, mortality, and nuptiality of 1926–30 was 1·019, the gross reproduction rate 1·175, and the gross reproduction rate of those who married 1·355. Counting 2·05 births for 1 female

average of three children per marriage, there must be many families of four or more to offset families of two or one and none at all. The problem of maintaining a population is, therefore, the problem of getting most people to have at least three children. This can only be done if a large number can be induced to have at least four. In other words, we have to make the four-child family fashionable.

This simple feature of the problem is almost universally neglected. Its importance is emphasized by what is actually happening in countries where the recorded statistics enable us to estimate what changes in the size of the family accompany a declining fertility. This has been done recently by Dr. Enid Charles in a memoir on the Australian population to be published in the near future. The decline has been accompanied by a proportionate increase of the two-child family over all others—including the one-child family. The implications of this fact are profoundly significant. Many people dismiss the urgency of the prospect discussed by asserting that most women want children. The problem of arresting a birth, the number of births necessary for replacement would be

$$\frac{1 \cdot 355}{1 \cdot 019} \times 2 \cdot 05 = 2 \cdot 73$$

Since mortality and nuptiality in England are pretty much the same as in Denmark, $2\frac{3}{4}$ births per married woman would also be sufficient in England (even if those who do not marry had no children at all).

decline at any level appropriate to circumstances is not merely, or mainly, the problem of inducing people who would otherwise have no children to have one or two. It has arisen mainly because people refuse to have children. It exists because the two-child family is now the fashionable family. The task of rational birth control is to make the four-child family fashionable. It exists because the whole influence of the birth-control movement has been exerted to exalt the two-child family as the social norm.

Travellers say that the anthropoid apes cannot count beyond four. Birth controllers are usually incapable of counting beyond two. That birth control advocates are quite sincere in professing that they do not want to stop people having children is beside the point. By exalting the two-child norm they have made the parent of the four-child family an object of public pity or opprobrium, liable to unfavourable comparison with an edible rodent universally detested in the southern hemisphere.

In adjusting themselves to facts about which there is no room for disagreement, many people find it difficult to disengage themselves from the nightmare of overpopulation. The possibility of overpopulation which haunted social reformers during the past century, is still taken seriously. This is partly due to ignorance concerning resources of power and substitutes which modern technology could make available for human welfare in a rationally planned economy. It may also take a more plausible form. Without contesting the potential of plenty which is now within reach, some advocates of birth control contend that there are too many people to be housed in genuine comfort. So up to a certain point a decline in population is welcome. That there is a psychological optimum of population density may well be true. Those of us who value privacy would be the last to deny it. This does not entitle us to overlook another consideration. As Enid Charles remarks, a pleasant scenic view half-way down a steep hill leading to a precipice is poor consolation to the driver of a car with no brakes.

Malthusian propaganda and the rather quaint physiology of Thomas Hardy's novels have conspired to inculcate a naïve teleology which invests parenthood with a perverse automatism. Human reproduction is assumed to proceed with its own momentum unless the most frantic propaganda is carried on to check it. That this is a travesty of ascertained facts about the social behaviour of the human species is easily seen when we examine the reasons which are casually given for the present character of population growth. It is also manifest in proposals sometimes advanced when those who welcome a decline in population are asked to state how they would arrest it at a level appropriate to their inclinations.

Two common reasons are given for the continuous

decline of fertility in northern and western Europe during the past fifty years. Professor Sargent Florence holds that it is due to the introduction of contraceptive devices. Taken by itself this is rather like saying that we wear clothes because sheep grow wool or silkworms secrete cocoons. The fact is that Fallopius wrote a treatise in the opening years of the seventeenth century on the commonest and safest appliance used to-day. It was advertised in England two centuries ago. What demands an answer is not what means people use to limit their families. It is what circumstances in their social lives lead them to use whatever means are available to them. The distinction is important because Hitler and Mussolini have also confused the means adopted with the end in view. Acting on the view taken by Professor Florence, they think that they can arrest the rapidly declining fertility of Germany and Italy by prohibiting particular methods of family limitation. History, which will record their failure, will read a new meaning in the adage that modern Love laughs at locksmiths.

The other reason—which is not advanced by serious students of the problem—is almost ubiquitous in general discussions of population. What makes people have less children is said to be *economic*. That is to say, people would be induced to have more children if they were more prosperous. The tenacity of this delusion is remarkable in view of the one feature of differential fertility familiar to most ordinary people. Putting the matter crudely, it is hardly too much to say that in the initial stages of declining fertility the richer people are, the less children they have. This is true through every grade of modern society except possibly of the negligibly over-rich. The one thing which is certain about the decline of fertility in contemporary civilization is that it is not due to economic obstacles in the ordinary sense of the term. That is to say, it is not due to limitations imposed by the *spending capacity of the individual parent*. Hence it is not surprising that the only radical remedy which has been widely favoured has been a conspicuous failure. Mr. Glass has recently published a résumé of existing schemes of family endowment in various countries. Up to date no scheme has provided a sufficient incentive to raise fertility.

The advocates of family endowment may make the objection that no allowances at present in force are big enough to achieve their object. Fortunately for their peace of mind, they do not venture to guess how big an inducement is necessary. A professional man who earns a thousand a year may be married to a woman earning a salary as high as his own. Nothing less than six hundred a year per child would maintain their joint standard of personal expenditure if they undertook to raise a family of four. Do the advocates of family endowment propose allowances on this scale within the economy of private profit, and have they any means of adjusting them to its concomitant inequalities of income? To ask the question is to supply the answer. The situation with which we are faced is one for which industrial capitalism offers no solution. A system of family allowances which could conceivably provide a sufficient stimulus to raise fertility above the extinction potential would wreck it.

Few who are Socialists will quarrel with this conclusion, and if there were nothing more to say there would be no reason for raising the issue in this context. The reason for doing so is that Socialists are still largely prejudiced by the Malthusian mythology and too easily assume that population will look after itself, if capitalism is abolished. Certain features of man's social behaviour are common to any kind of civilized society. For instance, we may presume that men and women will still wear clothes if a Socialist economy replaces capitalism. It is, therefore, a naïve error to welcome the admitted biological failure of capitalism, unless we are convinced that Socialism can ensure the irreducible minimum of fertility on which the permanence of civilized society depends. Sooner or later Socialists will have to face the following question. Is the pattern of sterility characteristic of declining capitalism wholly a consequence of social agencies inherent in capitalism as such, or is it in part or wholly a consequence of social agencies which could still operate under Socialism? If the answer to the first question is negative, a positive population policy is a paramount concern of Socialism.

There are some Socialists who will reply that Russia has no population problem. To dismiss the issue on these grounds is superficial if not flippant. Fertility which was higher in Russia than in any other European country before the war has actually declined since the Revolution. The recent restrictions on abortion do not encourage the belief that the present rulers of the u.s.s.r. are entirely happy about it. A generation must elapse before the data supplied by the Soviet Union itself can justify any rational judgment concerning the effect of present social policy on the attitude of parenthood. Meanwhile spending power is still low throughout the Union as a whole, the bulk of the population is not yet urbanized, and the study of differential fertility in other countries justifies the belief that Soviet industrialization is imitating many features propitious to sterility in the social structure of capitalist countries. For all these reasons the example of Russia can give us little guidance about the place of parenthood in a Socialist economy, more especially if it replaces capitalism at a stage when fertility is below the biological minimum. Before we could draw any conclusions from the Russian scene we should need to know how far Russia will proceed along the road to vocational equality in sex relations or whether the present headlong retreat to the patriarchal family is a temporary expedient, how far Soviet policy will favour a stable marriage relationship or whether easy divorce will be liquidated like abortion, how far the present enthusiasm for rapid industrialization will perpetuate the evils of urban congestion in capitalist countries or whether the demand for a modicum of decent privacy will assert itself as proletarian decorum. Even if we could yet answer these questions, the example of Russia would be of dubious significance. The psychological difficulties of raising fertility to the survival level when it has fallen far below it, may be immeasurably greater than checking its descent below the survival minimum when it is still at a much higher level.

In the meantime we have substantial materials for estimating what features of capitalist civilization are propitious to fertility or otherwise. So we can decide whether these need be perpetuated by a Socialist economy. The necessary data are supplied by the existence of wide differences in actual fertility and the rate at which it is declining in different communities, occupations, and localities within the same national units. Among the more relevant features which emerge from a survey of the phenomena of differential fertility are urban congestion, child labour, employment of women, stability of marriage, and low initial earnings in occupations with high maximal emoluments. Of these the most striking is the urban-rural fertility differential which is an almost universal feature of contemporary communities.

This is not a university lecture, and I do not propose to justify any of my subsequent remarks by columns of statistics. For the last six years I have been responsible for directing studies on population, some of them published and others not as yet available to the world at large. Inevitably I have arrived at some provisional conclusions in a field of research where much work remains to be undertaken before it will be legitimate to be dogmatic. The most I claim for the views which I shall state is that the tentative conclusions of a person who has made a study of the available data are more likely to be justified than the prejudices of those who know as much about them as Sir Arnold Wilson.

Among other features of differential fertility urban congestion claims pre-eminence, if only because it is not an essentially *new* feature of capitalist society. Some of the large cities of Europe were incapable of reproducing themselves long before a decline in national fertility began. Indeed, the past hundred years has seen the continual growth of the town at the expense of a higher level of fertility in the surrounding countryside. That high density of population generally goes with low fertility is beyond dispute. Difference of opinion only arises in the explanations offered for it. One view is that the relatively high fertility of the countryside is due to ignorance of contraceptive amenities. Before accepting this as a sufficient reason, we ought to ask why the conditions of life in a city favour the spread of contraceptive knowledge. In so far as urbanism favours low fertility, some conspicuous features of city life may be grouped under three headings: positive obstacles to parenthood inherent in the conditions of urban congestion, alternative distractions which compete with the satisfaction of the claims of parenthood as a source of enjoyment, and the impact of a new pattern of social relations on the stability of the family group.

The recognition of some of the positive obstacles presents no difficulties to parents themselves. It is only necessary to mention them because so few people are parents. Every mother of four knows that a garden surrounded by a wall is worth all the labour-saving devices yet invented. You may provide crèches, school feeding, family allowances, holidays with pay for expectant mothers, and a thousand and one other inducements. If you do not give people space you will not make parenthood endurable. As a parent, I have no doubt whatever in asserting that five children in a house surrounded by its own garden in a locality where there is little traffic are far less trouble than one child in a London flat. It is my deliberate opinion that flat life is incompatible with fertility, and if Socialists cannot think of anything better than the Workers' Flats in Vienna, we should be thankful that Dolfuss destroyed them before they had built sterility into the structure of a Socialist Society.

A second feature of urban life is sometimes dismissed too lightly because bishops are apt to make tiresome remarks about it. The drift of the population from country to town involves a continual displacement of active enjoyment by passive forms of satisfaction. For people who find their amusements in cultivating roses, growing their own salads, keeping bees or breeding rabbits in their own gardens, playing the piano, making their own clothes and household amenities, the use of leisure does not conflict with the demands of the home as the centre of family life. These pursuits are either impossible under urban conditions or disappear in competition with the *passive* distractions which city life offers. The cinema, which could be the greatest instrument yet devised for democratizing knowledge, if every mathematical classroom were fitted with a projector, is mainly used to compensate the unbearable tedium of life in a model flat. Crowds assemble to watch games which are only played by experts or gentlemen. Having abandoned the family pew and the choir practice, we turn on the radio and listen to crooners.

Side by side with the commercialization of passive enjoyment children and parents compete with one another in maintaining a pattern of conspicuous expenditure. This being so, it is not surprising that no system of family allowances yet devised has encouraged people to have more children. The chief use of an income in modern life is to purchase substitutes for whatever satisfaction parenthood brings.

The pattern of *passive satisfaction* and *conspicuous expenditure* encouraged by an increasing multiplicity of useless commodities and new distractions is only one side of the psychological problem presented by urban concentration. In rural surroundings where children grow up in contact with the recurrence of parenthood in animals and plants the processes by which life renews itself are accepted as natural events. In the city reproduction is an unwarranted intrusion of hospital practice on the orderly routine of a mechanized existence. The machine, which neither grows nor begets, sets the fashion of human relationships. In the large community the family ceases to function as a focus for social relations, as the individual is free to choose associates more and more exclusively from persons of the same occupational and age groups.

One feature of the large community of conspicuous expenditure is of special interest in connection with the social class with the lowest fertility. This is the culture value which is increasingly attached to foreign travel. Perhaps no characteristic of modern life is more devastating to the stability of the family group. Within the professional class, whose

184

fertility is now well below a 50 per cent replacement level, a married couple are faced by the deliberate choice between repudiating parenthood and accepting a cultural standard despised by other members of their occupational group. Familiarity with the names of Viennese hotels and a liberal smattering of un-English tags collected on vacational tours are now the indispensable stigmata of an educated person in a milieu where discussion of homosexuality excites less disgust than a reference to homework or whooping-cough. We are rapidly approaching a state of affairs in which the cultural barriers between the fertile and the infertile within one and the same social class are as acute as any pre-existing barriers between contiguous social classes.

What significance we attach to the employment of women under urban conditions outside the home raises the most difficult issues which a rational population policy will have to face, and they may be left for discussion at a subsequent stage. Here it is sufficient to state that the social accompaniments of low fertility suggested by existing differences connected with locality and occupation are not necessarily restricted to a capitalist economy. To some extent, perhaps very largely, they are characteristic of industrialism rather than of capitalism as such. The laudable project of relieving us from the dictatorship of the banks or the parasitism of the rentier of itself offers no guarantee that they will disappear.

Indeed, the study of population compels us to make a distinction between two radically different types of Socialist planning. One may be called planning for survival, the other planning for purchasing power. These alternatives have nothing to do with any schisms which separate Socialists on matters of political strategy. Whatever views Socialists may hold on matters of party allegiance, most of them are now mainly concerned with the same main objective. They aim at keeping productive efficiency at a maximum by expanding the volume of effective demand through social control of production and remuneration. In other words, they are less concerned with asking whether capitalist industrialism produces the things men need most than with demanding that everyone should have access to the goods it is capable of producing.

Because of the rising popularity of Fascist doctrines, to which I shall allude later, it is important to emphasize that the distribution of purchasing power to increase the volume of effective demand is essentially different from the view held by the pioneers of Socialism fifty or a hundred years ago. It would have been regarded by them as a capitulation to the prevailing doctrine of *laissez-faire*, against which they revolted. Men like Owen and Morris were far less taken in by the glamour of capitalism than we are. They were not content to criticize it because it distributed its products unjustly or because it was incapable of producing as large a quantity of goods as a planned economy could deliver. They also, and more especially, attacked it because it was not producing the kind of goods which are good for people to want and to strive for. They were not hypnotized by the liberal delusion that things people have been educated to demand by capitalist advertisement are necessarily the things they need most.

To-day we are apt to dismiss their lament on the ugliness which capitalist enterprise has bequeathed us as mere aestheticism with no significance for a realistic political programme. What is called realism implies a servile acceptance of the three cardinal errors of early capitalist ideology. The first is the assumption that the greatest good of the greatest number is achieved by producing the greatest number of saleable goods and ensuring that the greatest number of people can take their choice. The second is that the large community is a necessary condition of high productive capacity. The third is that peace between nations can only be ensured by maximum division of labour with free trade. I believe that each of these postulates is sociologically false, and that the results of acting as if they were true will be biologically disastrous. If Socialism accepts the distribution of purchasing power as its primary and sole concern its success will merely aggravate the tendencies which have made capitalism a biological failure. Meanwhile it will not disarm criticism by capitulating to Liberal ideals. On the contrary, its preoccupation with an exclusively mechanical conception of scientific planning will make it easier for the fake biological doctrines of Fascism to canalize discontents which are more deep-seated than many of us realize, and more widespread than poverty alone.

Neither of these results need occur if Socialists are prepared to undertake a more radical critique of the social values which capitalism has imposed on us. The Liberal ideology which has replaced the penetrating insight of the pioneers of English Socialism was adapted to the characteristics of capitalist development in an age when the chief source of power was coal, the sole instrument of chemical manufacture was heat, the basic constituents of metallurgical operations were iron and copper, the only method of quick transit was the train, and the principal capital asset of agriculture was the land itself. We are now on the threshold of an age of hydro-electric power, of electrolytic chemical processes, of light metals which exist in abundance everywhere. Cellulose is beginning to displace coal as a source of synthetic operations. Fertilizers, tank-culture, and applied genetics have made land the least important part of capital equipment in food production. Civil aviation, the light car, television, and broadcasting provide an escape from the disadvantages of cultural isolation contingent on small community life. Urban congestion is unnecessary. A much higher potential of self-sufficiency exists, and the advent of a light metal economy will remove one of the principal sources of national rivalries. In these circumstances the Labour Party can think of nothing better than perpetuating the effete technology of coal by nationalizing the mines, tinkering with London's transport facilities, putting up flats in flowerless streets for two-child families, and bleating about the nationalization of the land without advancing a single contructive proposal for collectivizing the nation's food supply on a scientific basis.

To this the practical politician will reply that the Labour Party has to take its marching orders from the trade unions, as the National Government has to pipe the tune for which the Bank of England pays. This is not realism. It is mere laziness. One country after another is submitting to the lure of leadership and the totalitarian principle. They will continue to do so, if the spokesman of democracy renounces his responsibility to educate his constituents and accepts the inevitability of compromise between sectional interests. Even the much-despised aestheticism of the Utopians is being vindicated by events. In his own time Morris contended that the drabness of capitalism is its chief condemnation. Hitler has now shown that people will go without butter if you give them circuses. Morris was a sound social psychologist in recognizing that a Socialist programme cannot afford to neglect the fact that people want their lives to be picturesque. He was a sound biologist in believing that we could make Britain so beautiful that people would neither need nor wish to travel. If we are to plan for survival our first aim must be to create a social environment in which the setting of the family is satisfying because it is also picturesque. It may be that the mere survival of Socialism as a movement will demand the same reorientation of social values. The Dictator countries have already shown that national survival is a slogan which will drive people to the polls. If we neglect the significance of this fact Socialism may make way for the circus man with the short moustache and the long whip.

So far I have emphasized one aspect of the social background of sterility. I have suggested that if Socialism accepts the *large-community of conspicuous expenditure*, the advent of a Socialist economy will serve only to make the decline of population more certain, more swift, and more irretrievable. On the other hand, there is no reason why Socialism should identify scientific planning with an exclusively mechanical technology, and the urban pattern which moulded the social *mores* of capitalism when mechanical technology was based on coal as a source of power, of chemical manufacture and of chemical synthesis. While the urban-rural fertility differential directs attention to many features of town life which are inimical to parenthood, it does not supply all the information we need for a survival policy. To arrest the decline of a population at any appropriate level it may be necessary to apply simultaneously a very large number of expedients each of which of itself would have very little influence.

The employment of women has already been mentioned as a feature associated with fertility below the survival minimum. I have expressed the opinion that family allowances on a scale compatible with capitalist distribution applied within the framework of capitalist production are not likely to guarantee survival. This does *not* mean that family endowment can be dropped out of the programme of a Socialist economy. When civilized countries recognize the menace of racial extinction, women may well be able to dictate their own terms. So I do not think it is profitable for a male to speculate upon what their terms will be. From the masculine standpoint one consideration is obvious. It is a monstrous injustice to expect men to undertake the sole financial responsibility of parenthood and agree to equal pay for equal work. The attempt to induce the male population to co-operate in maintaining its continued existence is not likely to succeed in a society which endorses equal pay for equal work without paying for the cost of rearing a family.

From the feminine point of view it is difficult to see how a system of family endowment can be made to work if remuneration for parenthood is less than for other forms of socially useful activity. Hence planning for survival may entail a much closer approximation to equality of wealth than most Socialists now advocate. During the last few years we have witnessed what appeared to be a headlong retreat from the equalitarian view in the Soviet Union. The system of bonuses for motherhood introduced during the past year may provide a new illustration of progress by the interpenetration of opposites, and Equality, lately denounced as a social democratic deviation, may be reinstated as proletarian virtue. In pursuing our own line to the Equalitarian commonwealth, we must either rehabilitate the Socialist creed in alignment with the evident biological failure of the Acquisitive Society, or allow the population issue to become a new bulwark of social reaction. There are sufficient signs that the Conservative Party is more alive to its existence than the Labour Party. This is the inevitable consequence of selecting our Radical Intellegentsia from the products of a moribund culture and conducting Socialist propaganda in a way which inevitably antagonizes people equipped with scientific and technical knowledge.